IF I LIVE TO TELL

A True Story
by Akeela Hayder Green

with Michael Minkoff, Jr.

THE LIBERTY ALLIANCE
Powder Springs, Georgia

IF I LIVE TO TELL

by Akeela Hayder Green
with Michael Minkoff, Jr.

Published by:

> The Liberty Alliance
> 3150-A Florence Road, Suite 2
> Powder Springs, GA 30127–5385
> www.LibertyAlliance.com

Scripture quotations from The Holy Bible, New Century Version®. Copyright © 2005 by Thomas Nelson, Inc. Used by permission. All rights reserved.

Printed in the United States of America.

Text design: Michael Minkoff, Jr.
Cover design: Kent Jensen of Knail Design <*www.knail.com*>
Cover photos: iStockphoto (portrait) / Masterfile (glass)
Back cover bio photo: Amy Hiner Vallorani <*www.AmyVallorani.com*>

ISBN: 978-1-4675-3926-5

WARNING:
Some content may be inappropriate for children. Reader discretion is advised.

Contents

Acknowledgements

I FEEL SO MANY PEOPLE HAVE been a part of making this book happen, and I want to thank them all:

Brandon Vallorani,

This book would not have been possible without your support and belief in me. If not for your suggestion, I wouldn't have even thought publishing this book was a possibility. I will always feel blessed to know you. *Thank you* is not enough for all you bring to my life. I can never repay you, but forever I will hold you with undying loyalty in the highest place of respect. I promise you this. I love you and feel blessed by God that I can call you my brother in Christ and in life.

Michael Minkoff,

This book would still be little scribbled notes on jumbled pages if you weren't an exceptional writer and, honestly, an amazing person. I am honored that you have exercised your God-given talent for me, and this book sings your praises, as do I. You have the purest of hearts, and I know how tough this was for you to do! In love and friendship, I thank you deeply.

Arthur Fretwell,

My life coach, my friend, and my confidant, you are truly dear to my heart. You gave me the push I needed to actually make this book happen. Without you, I wouldn't have had the courage to speak out and share this! Thank you for all that you do for me and all you are.

My dear children Max and Lily,

The love I have for you is the purest love I've ever known. You are the reason I breathe, the reason I'm still here fighting, and why my heart is still beating. You both are the glue that holds the pieces of it together. My love for you both will never be matched. I'm proud to be your mom and your friend. I hope all I've been through makes me a better mom.

Foreword

My purpose for this book is not to make accusations or receive pity, to achieve justice for myself or to uncover other people's shame. I have not sugar-coated the truth, nor have I exaggerated it. This is an honest account of my trials and the victory I gained through them.

I want to put this book out into the world for many reasons—some selfish and some selfless.

First, this book was the cheapest therapy in the world! It enabled me to unburden myself of things I had pushed deep down into my soul and left to fester. It gives me such relief now that I have brought this all into the light. I have not shared this story with very many people, and I would honestly be embarrassed to tell it to you in your presence. Writing it into a book may have been the only way possible for me to let go of this poison I have had in me for so many years. I feel such a sense of closure now, and at least for that reason, I think this book has been a success.

Second, I feel compelled to share my life if only to reach one victim with hope or lift up just one broken heart. I don't feel important enough to have an autobiography so to speak, but this is more than just *my* story. This is the story of countless victims around the world. But many of these victims have no hope, only despair. And I am sharing my life with the prayer that my journey might give even one of them the strength to carry on.

I would love to hear from anyone who benefits from reading this book. I want to know that the tragedies of my life have made a difference in this world for the better. I would love to have a greater assurance that the purpose of my life reaches beyond just my own satisfaction and happiness. I wanted to share my story with the world for just this reason.

I hope and pray no one ever has to endure anything like what is recounted in these pages. But if you have gone through or are going through something similar, I hope this book will reach you and strengthen you. Don't give up! There is a purpose to all of this. Trust me. If I can come through all of this and still find fulfillment and significance, then I know you can too.

After you read this book, look up to heaven and say thank you for your trials. They make you grateful for your blessings. They shape and mould you into the person you need to be to fulfill your unique purpose.

In painful times, I used to scream at God, *Why? Why me? When will this end?* If all I've been through, tough as it is to share, brings one person faith or hope to fight, then God has given me my answer. I went through all of this so I could live to tell the world that God is good all the time—even in our suffering.

Akeela Hayder Green
January, 2013
Dallas, Georgia

IF I LIVE TO TELL

Wish good for those who harm you; wish them well and do not curse them. Be happy with those who are happy, and be sad with those who are sad. Live in peace with each other. Do not be proud, but make friends with those who seem unimportant. Do not think how smart you are. If someone does wrong to you, do not pay him back by doing wrong to him. Try to do what everyone thinks is right. Do your best to live in peace with everyone. My friends, do not try to punish others when they wrong you, but wait for God to punish them with his anger. It is written: "I will punish those who do wrong; I will repay them," says the Lord. But you should do this:

> If your enemy is hungry, feed him;
> if he is thirsty, give him a drink.
> Doing this will be like pouring burning coals on his head.

Do not let evil defeat you, but defeat evil by doing good.

Romans 12:14–21

Prologue

IT SEEMED LIKE EVERY HOUSE in Iraq had a small entryway with a phone hanging on the wall—the only phone in the house, the old rotary kind with a wheel and finger holes. Calls were rare. Neighbors sometimes used the phones as a convenient way to chat, but these conversations had to be guarded. Someone was always listening. A few weeks back, a man down the street had called his neighbor, and in the course of their conversation, he had relayed a harmless joke about Saddam Hussein. The next day, the comedian was shot in the head in the street.

I had been in Iraq for a year already before I finally heard from my father. My dad had said my "vacation" to Iraq would last two weeks. He had finally decided to split up with his girlfriend, and things would be crazy. He wanted me to get to know his family anyway, and he also needed me out of the way for a little while so he could set up a new house for us. *Two birds with one stone.* I thought I might be able to help him. I was fifteen after all. He wouldn't hear it. It would be better this way, he said.

So there I was, still in Iraq, believing more every day that I would never leave. I was living at my Aunt Fareeda's house then. I stood in her dusty entryway with my back to a mirror. I clung to the thin sound of my father's voice, relayed as it was through countless connections from England to Iraq, probably being monitored by some distant Iraqi official, an electric lifeline to my old life—my old self, whoever that had been.

I had to be careful what I said for more than just the obvious reasons. I could not afford to test my father's temper. I also

5

couldn't afford to waste this opportunity. This might be the last time I talked to him. If I were ever going to get out of this place, I had to convince him that things were going very badly for me here.

But he didn't want to hear that. He had sent me to live in an embellished memory of his childhood—one of white marble floors and polished brass gates; palm trees and pomegranates and sultan's opulence. But one can't live in a memory, especially not one as inaccurate as all that. Things were probably never the way he remembered them, and they had only gotten worse since: blockades, wars, famines, and tyranny had all but consumed whatever comforts Iraq had once boasted. A thin trickle of black market goods was all that gave the common Iraqi any relief. That is, *if* out-of-country friends and family sent the money required to purchase things.

I couldn't tell him all that was on my mind. I had blocked so many of the details. What remained was a featureless void, a sinking feeling in the pit of my stomach that had no voice. Not that my father could hear it anyway. After a few minutes of my best attempt at small talk, I finally asked,

"Dad, how long am I going to be here?"

The question caught him off guard. I had removed any accusation from my tone, but he received my question as an attack anyway.

"Why? You should be happy there. What is there to come back to? Don't I send enough money to take care of you?"

"Yes, of course, Dad. I just didn't expect to be here for this long."

"Well, you must stay. Until you learn to cook. To keep house. To learn the customs of my family. You will stay until you become a good Iraqi woman."

There was no more I could do. When I hung up the phone, cut that tenuous connection, I felt like the last tether had been severed, and I was now lost, drifting out to sea like so much wreckage. I turned in the entryway and caught sight of myself in the mirror. I stopped and stared. This woman. Her hair was matted and thinning, still falling out in clumps. Her eyes bloodshot and clouded over. Her cheeks caved in. Her expression blank. Her lips straight, thin, and set—with resignation, not with resolve.

Is this what you wanted, father? Is this what a good Iraqi woman looks like?

"I will forgive them for the wicked things they did,
and I will not remember their sins anymore."

Hebrews 8:12

I: An English Girl

I GREW UP IN MANCHESTER, ENGLAND, a drab, industrial city on the way to seemingly any other place people would rather be: York or the north country or the like. It's a through-city, not a destination. But not for me. For me, it was home.

My father was Iraqi by birth, but he had become a typical Englishman long before I was born. In a way, he was two people. Very occasionally while I was growing up, his Arabic friends or family would come to our house for a visit and my father would put on his Iraqi self like it was a set of dress clothes he kept in a chest at the foot of his bed.

My English father drank heavily and cursed like he was in the Queen's navy. His Iraqi self was sober and pious. I didn't see it then as hypocrisy. To me, it was exotic and intriguing: how these men would grasp each other by the back of the necks to kiss and embrace; how they barked at each other in their harsh, one-volume language—I would have thought they were arguing if it hadn't been for the panting toothy smiles.

My father would present me to his Arabic companions like a stash of silver he had traded for some silk in a hard-fought bargain with the crafty West. And they would shout some jovial pronouncement over me in Arabic and palm both of my cheeks looking down on me with proud eyes. I would turn to my father for a translation. He would stumble over the words in broken English. He couldn't translate well, and it made sense. There was such a fixed wall between those two parts of himself, and he found it impossible to climb.

WHEN YOU'RE YOUNG, YOU DON'T see anything for what it is because you have nothing to compare it to. I thought my life was normal, and all the things in it typical. We didn't get out much, so this mistaken impression stuck with me longer than it sticks with most children.

My father never got along with my half-brother Troy, though he felt it his duty to provide for him. My mother had been all but disowned because of Troy. It was bad enough to my mother's mother, Nana, that my mother was having a baby out of wedlock. It was worse that the father was black. My dad felt the same way. He never shook the deep-set cultural belief that Africans were slaves, and he treated Troy as such. My mother fiercely protected Troy; he was always her favorite.

When my parents met, my mother needed someone to provide for her, and it was a bonus that my father, with his dark skin, might pass for Troy's father. My father needed citizenship, and it was a bonus that my mother was beautiful. Their marriage had passion too, even if it was the destructive and capricious kind. They met each other with material needs that marriage could fill. They didn't realize that filling those needs would also blot out their reasons to be married. By the time I was old enough to think about it, I had no idea what could have drawn my parents together.

Blond-haired, blue-eyed, and fair-skinned, my mother was a stark contrast to my father's green eyes and dark features. She was impetuous, independent, demanding, and hard. Layla, six years younger than I, the baby, was more like her—looked like her and acted more like her. I was daddy's little girl, his princess. He gave me his green eyes, olive skin, and black hair. He gave me his mother's name, Akeela. My mother envied everything he gave me.

My parents fought a lot. Their shouting contests provided the soundtrack of our childhood. I suppose if they had argued in Arabic, we could have pretended they were having a pleasant conversation about the weather.

It was never clear who started the arguments. It seemed they never started. Or ended. They'd submerge for a time while other things needed to get done, but they never got resolved. It was as if my parents had started The Great Argument soon after they married, and it was the only thing that stayed constant in their relationship. Over their numerous separations culminating in divorce, followed by their subsequent reunions and mostly final parting of ways, the Great Argument remained.

It had many battles. Over Troy. Over how I got things the other children didn't get. Over how my father worked too much. Over finances. They could pitch a battle over any issue. And they did.

There was violence too. Stairs were involved. My father dragged my mother by her hair up some stairs at his shop, in front of his employees. And her words begged for violence: every verbal jab like an electrode to an agitated bull. She knew she would get the upper hand if only he would hit her. *Then* she would make him sorry.

My mother was violent with him too. I remember one time particularly. My father had just bought a cellar-style wine bar, and it was opening night. My parents were separated at the time, but my mother came anyway. More than likely to try to sour the occasion for my father. She succeeded.

She met him at the entrance, and the Great Argument quickly commenced again. She won this skirmish, capping off a shouting match by shoving my father down the concrete stairs that led to his new business. I can see her standing at the top of the stairs, haughty and triumphant. When my father pushed himself up onto his hands and knees, were the doors already open to his first customers? I wonder how he saved face when he made his rounds that night, the perfect host in his black Italian suit, now scuffed at the knees. Did he cover his limp as best he could as he approached the tables to ask how everything was?

My mother had done her best to stain his successes with shame. But I imagine my father was able to put it out of his mind quickly enough. Quickly enough to infuriate her all the more. Is this what drew them back together? The dim prospect that they might be able to break the other once and for all?

I guess no one thought it odd that my father, a Muslim, should own a wine bar, though it was kind of like a Jew running a pig farm. My father owned many businesses. He always had an electrical store of some kind—selling and repairing appliances, distributing parts to electricians. When he first married my mother, he had almost nothing. He picked up broken appliances from the scrapyard—ovens, heaters, washers, dryers—and he would get the parts they needed, fix them, and resell them. He saved enough money from doing this that he was able to buy his first shop. No matter where he went, he always had at least one electrical shop, a constant reminder of where he came from.

He was smart with his money, and he started, bought, and sold many businesses while we were growing up. Most of them made money. My father loved to work. It's rational. *More in* usually means *more out*. Family life was different, especially with my mother. He's an idiot when it comes to relationships. Mostly because he treats them like just another business venture. He avoided his troubles at home by throwing himself into his work. He would take the fruit of his labors to buy peace at home. It worked with the kids for a while. It never worked with my mother. She always had her own car, sometimes two. Fine things if she wanted them. It didn't matter.

When my mother met my father in Liverpool, she had nothing in her possession but a child to take care of. It was around that time that she started to battle a nervous depression. Maybe she thought the sole reason for her feelings of insecurity was that she didn't have enough money to buy the things she and Troy needed. My dad could fix that, but then this didn't fix anything. Most people who don't believe in stuff they can't touch get really puzzled when they have way more than they need and still aren't satisfied. My mother needed something my father had no capacity to provide, but she never forgave him for letting her down.

MY PARENTS SEPARATED MANY TIMES before and after their divorce. Things were particularly bad in those times. Troy and I became unwitting soldiers in our parents' war. My father showered me with gifts almost to spite my mother who saw me more and more as my father's representative in her house.

We would be sitting at the table or something and she would look over at me with one eye, a lit cigarette in the corner of her mouth forcing her to close the other. I might smile at her. She would exhale a thin stream of smoke, tap off her ash with one practiced movement, and look at me squarely. She had a tendency to grind her teeth when she talked:

"You look just like your father. So ugly. You look just like the devil."

She said things like that so many times. Most of the hurts I endured as a child didn't reach me really. But these encounters with my mother did. Still trying to wrestle my identity out of the tangles of innocence and experience, I had no defense for her attacks. She was supposed to be my guardian. My guide.

I didn't understand then that, in my mother's eyes, I was just a way for her to hurt my father—to continue the Great Argument. If only I had been able to keep my mind focused on this one truth: *She means that for my father. She means that for my father.* I didn't realize that seeing me happy filled her with resentment and bitterness: *I'm sure he's very happy. Happy with another woman while I raise these kids. Happy with his work while I waste away, waiting on his scraps like a dog.*

My mother was a master of self-pity, but she did not exercise any other form. I felt her pain as well as my own whenever she attacked me, and it deformed my spirit. *If only I could do better. I just need to try a little harder. Maybe then she will love me.*

But except for these, I had very little other kinds of interactions with my mother. And it didn't seem to matter what I did. I couldn't please her. If all this bitterness was meant for my father, what then was left for me?

MY FATHER TREATED ME LIKE a princess when I was young. *His princess.* I went shopping with him almost every week, even when my parents were separated. He bought me girly things— pink and plastic things—candy, clothes, and the like. He loved to spend money on me, and I believed he loved me. My father had little else than money to invest in our relationship, or any other relationship for that matter, but he liked the bond he had with his little princess. Maybe because it was a more successful business venture than his long boarded-up marriage.

Things started to change in our relationship shortly after I was old enough to go to school. On my first day, my father planned to drop me off at primary school on his way to work. I rode beside him in my uniform, the back of my knees below my pleated skirt sticking slightly to the vinyl of the passenger seat in his white work van.

It smelled like engine grease and melted plastic, manly smells of my father's trade. There were no windows or seats in the back, only shelves on either side with countless new and used parts with purposes unknown to me, all smudged more or less with the same very fine black dust.

I was terrified of school. Of the variables in it. I imagined the teachers barking and sulking, clones of my parents. And I preferred to—how did Hamlet put it?—*bear those ills I have, than fly to others that I know not of.*

When the van pulled up to the entrance, I looked to my father. He did not exercise any form of pity, self or otherwise. He looked over at me evenly, and then after a moment, a clear, single expression formed in his eyebrows as if to say, "Well? Get on with it then." I wanted to cry, but I didn't. I would be a good girl for my father. *His princess.*

I opened the door to the van and slid down to the asphalt that bordered the white concrete walkway leading up to the school's entrance: big glass double doors with chrome hardware. I began to plod to the entrance, each of my feet little black leather boats on uncharted waters. I shot my head around quickly to see if my father was still there. He was looking in my direction from across my now empty seat, but his mind was already elsewhere. He was just waiting for me to become someone else's responsibility so he could get on to work—the tasks of his day already forming an orderly queue. I finally got to the entrance. A teacher pushed open a door, and the sounds of the place came over me. So many voices, and so much bustle. I completely lost my resolve. I turned to look at my father one last time as the door closed me in, but his van was pulling away and I could no longer see his face.

Without his presence, I had no reason to behave. I didn't have to be strong for him anymore. He wasn't there. I stood at the door, my palms fogging the glass, and I cried out for him over and over again. At intervals, my voice would rise in pitch and volume into screams. I became even louder whenever a teacher tried to touch me. I would not be comforted. I did not want to be here. I wanted my Daddy.

They had little choice but to call my father at work. I was so relieved when I saw his van pull up, but I realized as soon as I saw his face what I had done. I had seen that face before. Mostly pointed at my mother. His brow was all knotted and there was a tightness in his voice when he talked to the teacher at the entrance:

"I'm so sorry. This won't happen again."

No. He was going to make sure of it. He led me to the parked van, his hand vise tight on my shoulder. He opened one of the double doors on the back and pushed me inside, slamming the door behind us. He pushed me over his knee. I heard the tinkle of his belt unfastening and his voice growing louder and more incoherent. I can't remember what he said. The violence of his voice convinced the words to quit meaning. And they crashed against me together as the belt buckle bit into my skin over and over again. His fingers held like steel, his voice was a fire, his legs a chair of asphalt. His whole person was unyielding. These were the ills I knew.

I retreated within myself. I didn't have my father's walls. I didn't have my mother's siege works. I didn't have the tools to wage this war or to defend myself. But I had a labyrinth in my heart. And no one could find me there.

Then he stopped. He left me in the back of the van. There was a partition between the cabin and the back with a little rectangular window in it. He drove all the way to the shop without saying anything to me. I tried not to sob, but I could feel my chest heaving with stuttering breaths. With every breath, I smelled my father's work, his true love. Like it was taunting me. I could see him through the window. He was locked up to me—his face fixed, both hands on the wheel, cool and distant.

When we got to his shop, he called my mother. I could hear the mosquito whines of her electric voice in the receiver next to his ear, but I could not make out any of her words. I heard only my father's side of the conversation.

"Sheree. You have to come get Akeela now."

. . .

"No. She's here at the shop. She went ape shit at the school. Wonder where she gets *that*. I had to leave work to go get her."

. . .

"Do you think *I* expected to have her? I have work to do. You're her mother. Come and get her *right fucking now*."

. . .

"Fine. I'll handle it."

. . .

"Just forget it. I said I'd *deal with it*."

He hung up. My father turned to me, and motioned for me to follow him. He led me to a stairwell and started climbing the stairs two at a time, stopping occasionally without a word to let me almost catch up before he began climbing again. I followed him, staring at the wooden stairs and my black shoes against them. I couldn't bear to look at his face.

He took me to the fifth floor of his building—an unfinished flat. When I stepped over the threshold, he looked down at me, black against the only light on that floor—a naked bulb that hung from the ceiling—its radiance splintering at his edges.

"Stay here 'til you calm down."

He shut the door. Shut out the light. I heard the door bolt from the outside, that sound of metal sliding against metal. I stood alone in the dark. I didn't dare sit on the floor. I felt for the wall. It was brick, with the sloppy mortar between the bricks frozen in bulges. I put my arm against the rough wall, leaned my face onto my arm. At first my ears, taking over for my useless eyes, focused on the miniature sounds, and my anxious imagination filled in gaps. First, my father's shoes tapping the concrete, shuffling down the stairs and away. Then the throaty *coo* and wing-flutter of pigeons. The chitter and scuttle of rodents. The almost imperceptible clicks of skittering insects—crickets, roaches, and centipedes. Probably spiders. And longer sounds in the belly of the building—hums and drones—ominous and undying.

I started screaming, my throat already raw from before. I called out for him over and over again, then just started shrieking. I started to feel dizzy in the dark with no point of reference, my knees locked. I was retreating within myself again. It was easier this time. My eyes were open and adjusted to the darkness, but I stopped trying to see. I could hear, but I stopped listening. I became blank. My cries, still as loud and steady, became mechanical, no longer hoping for comfort, but still crying for it.

I was there for two hours. It felt longer.

My mother came to collect me. She led me downstairs, and passed by my father with a self-righteous air. His day had been going better. The two hours had passed quickly for him, no doubt. *So much to do.* When we got outside, one of my father's employees, Dave, stopped us.

"I'm so glad you came. I had no idea what to do. She was just up there screaming, and I didn't know what else to do."

"You did the right thing. Thank you."

"Yeah. I just thought, 'I can't work like this!' You know? And that bastard wasn't doing anything. Nothing. And I didn't know what he had done to her. But he just left her in there. I can't work like that, you know. So I called you."

"Well, thanks for doing what you did. You don't know what that man puts us through. So hard for us. For these kids."

"Can I help at all?"

"No. There's nothing that can be done. I have to see this through. For the kids. You should just quit. We have to endure it. But you don't."

"Yeah? I think I might. I can't work for a man like that, right?"

My mother smiled, satisfied. I thought she would be upset with me once we got in the car, but on the way home, she seemed almost happy. She didn't talk to me, but I could see she was formulating a monologue for the blowup she was going to have with Dad later. I could see the familiar words on her face like a scrolling marquee as she savored them:

Such a big man... beating the piss out of a helpless little girl. I bet you enjoyed doing it too. Especially in her little schoolgirl outfit. You pig. Wouldn't be surprised if she winds up a junkie or a whore. Then half-dead on your doorstep with a little bastard in tow. And it'll be your fault. Don't come crying to me then. You're as bad a father as you are a husband. You treat us like trash. Even your favorite. You treat her like trash too. You disgust me. You're a terrible father. You couldn't even make it a few hours without my help. If it weren't for me, these kids might as well not have any parents. I've sacrificed my whole life for them. And you've done nothing...

MY PARENTS SPLIT UP SOON after. They got back together for just long enough to make Layla, and then they split up again. I don't even understand how they were intimate. But their relationship was rotten with passion, so I guess it was almost as easy to turn that passion to sex as to violence.

My father didn't know my mother was pregnant with Layla for a few months. Their temporary romance had dissipated like the fizz from stale champagne, and he was in his own place again, leaving Troy and me with my mother. She began to wage the Argument against me in earnest then. All the verbal barbs and poisonous looks she had stockpiled in the arms buildup of her cold marriage, she now let loose on me without fear of retaliation.

She was a depressive woman, and the powerful hormone cocktail her body brewed up during pregnancy sent her over the edge. She was crazy.

When my father found out she was pregnant, he moved back in for a time. *For the kids.* They fought more than ever. My mom thought her pregnancy was some kind of buffer against violence so she pushed my dad even harder than usual, just begging for blows. My mother always complained my father didn't support her emotionally. She tried everything she could to hurt him. Maybe if he hurt like she did, he would empathize with her. Finally feel something. She was mistaken. He would bear it for a time, then lash out. The only emotion he ever seemed to feel was anger. Maybe lust. If you can call that an emotion. I started to realize around this time a truth that has stuck with me since: *Hurt people hurt people.*

I HAD TO GO BACK to school eventually, of course. I didn't fit in at primary school, but I got used to it. My dad's lesson had sunk deep. I would never do that again. Ever. I had to try harder. Do everything I could to please him. It was easier to please my teachers. I found that I loved school. It was rational. If I worked hard, I got high marks and approval from my teachers. I poured myself into my studies like my father poured himself into work. I guess I was like him in some ways after all.

After I finished primary school, I was sent to a much less expensive high school in a shabbier part of town. I felt much more at ease there, but I stood out from the other kids. I spoke proper English and I followed the dress code more strictly than the more casual school enforced it.

School also introduced me to other species of adults. It turned out my teachers weren't clones of my parents. I had one teacher in particular, a homeroom teacher named Mr. Hutchins, who defined for me for the first time what a man should and could be like. He was well-built and tall, nurturing and supportive. He had a shiny bald head and black square-framed glasses. He made me feel smart. He would say, "What are you doing at a school like this?" He always took my side in those trivial disputes schoolchildren have over word usage and grammar.

"It's *mom*. Not *mum*. Right, Mr. Hutchins?"

"It's *may I*, not *can I*. Right, Mr. Hutchins?"

He was one of the first men to show me kindness, and I gravitated toward it. Starved at home for even the non-dairy creamer of human kindness, my still-developing self fed on his small and always appropriate attentions with eagerness. They gave me self-confidence and pluck in my core. I couldn't display these budding traits to my parents without retribution, so I hid them deep below the surface. I smiled rarely. I smiled a lot more when I was at school.

For most of this time, my parents were separated. They broke up again when Layla was one or two, and Dad started seeing other women. At least, that's what my mom thought. It gnawed at her. She took it out on me. I wasn't allowed to go anywhere but home after school. I wasn't allowed to talk to boys. My mother suspected

I did not follow these rules, so when I got home, she would force me to strip off my clothes and she would inspect every part of my body. She would smell my fingers to see if I had been smoking. She smelled my breath to see if I had been drinking. When I took a shower, she would come in and check my dirty underwear. Maybe she thought I was messing around with boys. I don't know. I was a little girl. I knew nothing of any of these things.

I was so embarrassed about my body, and terrified of my mother. I felt guilty the first time I had my period. I didn't tell my mother for two weeks. I thought I had done something wrong. Maybe that was what she was checking my underwear for. I wondered which one of my secret thoughts had triggered this new and frightening development. My mother laughed it off when I told her.

"Is that it?"

One day, when I was a few minutes late getting home from school, she beat me with a cast-iron poker. She didn't believe my story. She couldn't see me for who I was. She projected herself onto me. And she wasn't just satisfying her anger with my father. She was punishing herself too. I blamed myself. I would try to do better.

Then things got even worse. My Nana died of a brain hemorrhage, and the news crushed my mother's spirit. She had a nervous breakdown, withdrawing completely into her private world of manicured grief.

Her relationship with Nana had been complicated. Her mother had basically disowned her because of Troy. Really, they had a terrible relationship, but dead people tend to have their faults either eliminated or exaggerated to suit the needs of the living. As soon as Nana died, my mother acted like a great comfort had been removed from her life. Like she had been deprived of the only person in the world who really understood her. She always managed to make things about herself.

The week before Nana died, my mother tried to get me to visit her. Nana had just moved there to be closer to us, but I was reluctant to go. The only contact I had with Nana was on my birthday. My mother would take us all to her house. Nana bought me a candy bar and a doll. The same thing every year. I think these trips were more important to my mother than they were to us. She was too proud to try to visit her mother on her own, but we kids gave her the chance to be available should Nana finally decide to show her some sign of forgiveness. But Nana was not the forgiving kind.

One year, my mother left me there overnight the day before my birthday so I could visit with Nana. I didn't want to be there. Nana had been a nomadic gypsy, and she struck me as hidden and dark. She believed hardness was the best policy. That life did not favor the soft. I was at her window pouting. I told her I did not want to stay there.

"Don't you want your birthday presents?"

"I don't care. I just want to go home."

"Suit yourself, then." She said it without bitterness, cold as a hardwood floor in winter. And she took my birthday presents off the table and left the room.

I just didn't understand old age. The slow movements and cryptic, lingering stares of old people made me uneasy. To me, the aged must have been hiding their energies, and their motives. They were liable to lash out at any moment with their hidden vigor. When you least expected.

When my Nana died, I blamed myself. Maybe if I had just visited her, things would have been different. My mom would have taken me. Maybe she needed an excuse to visit Nana. Maybe I was that excuse. Had I robbed my mother of that last opportunity to make amends? Now she could never get forgiveness. Or give it. I had caused her nervous breakdown. I had to try harder.

Then my mother just stopped taking care of us. She would sit in a chair chain-smoking, like smoke could fill the emptiness inside her. She would sit there looking at the floor talking quietly to herself for hours. You'd ask her a question and it wouldn't register at all. You'd touch her arm, and she'd start and pull back with this terrified look in her face. The house was a mess, and there wasn't much to eat, but we just left her alone. She was gone. My father didn't know any of this was going on. He probably didn't want to know. Ms. Turner, the headmaster at our school, suggested that my mother send us away for a while.

"Just until you get yourself together."

She was too proud to ask my father to take us, so we went to foster care for a few months. And I thought, *This is my fault too.*

THE IRONICALLY-NAMED SHEPHERDS WERE OUR foster family. Ms. Turner brought us to their two-story brick house on a corner lot in a classic Manchester suburb. We walked into their foyer. Ms. Turner met Mrs. Shepherd there, introduced us, and then left after looking at each one of us, lingering a bit longer over Layla, who was about two.

Mrs. Shepherd looked at us with the faintest grimace. She swept it away quickly, then her face was all business. She took on the air of a roadside inn keeper. She showed us to our upstairs rooms, Layla and I in one, Troy in the other. Then she glided downstairs. She was a busy woman.

The house smelled musty and choked, like a hidden leak kept the close air well-supplied with mold spores. The house gave the impression of an unfinished basement. The colors of the decorations and furniture looked like they could *almost* work together, but didn't quite cohere: chestnut, chocolate, and umber browns with faded asparagus, dartmouth, and hunter greens. Clashing earth tones that belied the coldness of the house. A tapestry hung on visible nails in the upstairs hallway. It had the family name stitched into it in large flowing script, almost as if to remind the tenants: *This is not your home.* As if we needed the reminder.

Troy and I were ashamed to be there. We ducked behind a low wall near our mother's house after school waiting for our acquaintances to clear out. We didn't want to have to explain the situation. Foster care is for parentless chimney sweeps in Dickens novels, right? Our parents weren't dead. Sometimes I thought it would be better if they were. I felt bad for thinking that. *See, Akeela. If you wouldn't think such horrible things, maybe they wouldn't have sent you away.*

The Shepherds had two kids of their own, a boy and a girl. They too treated us like unwanted boarders. We rarely got to play on the swing set in the backyard. You know how kids are. They don't care about their toys unless someone else wants them. The Shepherd kids had never realized before just how much they adored their swing set until we got there.

Every day, Mrs. Shepherd cooked a delicious home-cooked meal: stuffed turkey and sausages, mashed potatoes, meat pies, hot buttered scones, and the like—English comfort food. Which we did not eat. We ate banana sandwiches at another table. Always banana sandwiches. I hated bananas. When I told Mrs. Shepherd that, she gave me an exasperated glare, reached down to my plate and picked the bananas off the bread. I ate the slimy bread, still tasting like bananas. I ate little more than bread while I was there, getting my daily meal at school. The Shepherds fed the leftovers to their dogs.

I realized then how some people pervert justice and duty. It may not have been their duty to show us love or to share their food, but why did they take such pleasure in withholding it from us? And all the while, they could fall back on, "We've always done our duty. We have given them far more than was justly due them."

Mr. Shepherd was indifferent to the proceedings of his house. He rarely peeped over his newspaper even at his own children. I doubt he noticed us at all—that we showed up or that we left.

At the time, I had thick, black curls that reached past my waist. Unruly and beautiful hair—one of the only parts of my appearance I took pride in. I remember people would stop my mother in the store or on the street to comment on it. It made me feel one-of-a-kind. My mother of course was annoyed with people for the attention I was getting, trying to be polite while she struggled with her jealousy.

Mrs. Shepherd took it upon herself to tame my hair, perhaps believing she could tame *me* in the process—the unkempt little stray she had taken into her home. She would sit me down on a wooden stool in front of a mirror in the upstairs bathroom and she would drag a stiff-toothed brush from my roots all the way to my ends, pulling out hair the whole way. If I let my head jerk with the movement of the brush or cried out in pain, she would thwack the back of my head.

"Be still. And *be quiet*... It doesn't hurt."

Then she would continue with the same hurried strokes. This ritual could have been a time of bonding. But it wasn't. Mrs. Shepherd was not the motherly type.

She seemed kinder to Layla, who was still young enough to be fooled by fake shows of kindness. She took more time to be a mother to her, though her attempts were often cruel. She hid

Layla's pacifier, which Layla depended on to go to sleep. That first night, my baby sister cried out for it in our room. I approached Mrs. Shepherd to enlist her help in finding it.

"Do you know where Layla's dummy is?"

"Aren't you supposed to be in bed?"

"Yes, ma'am. But Layla can't sleep without her dummy. Do you know where it is?"

"Yes. I have it."

"Well, Layla needs it."

"She does *not* need it. She's much too old for it. Now go back to bed. She'll stop crying eventually."

"But…"

"No buts. Go to bed."

They didn't bother even pretending to be kind to Troy and me. They treated Troy with special disdain, like he was a half-breed in their eyes, an abomination. We were beyond help. They collected the money to put us up. They weren't being paid to be our parents. Or to be kind.

After a few months, my father finally found out what was going on. He was furious. He blamed my mother. She blamed him. He decided he needed to move back in. Make another attempt. *For the kids.* It didn't last.

I WAS ABOUT TWELVE WHEN we moved into the last house my parents tried to live together in. They were already divorced. My father had just sold two businesses, so money was always at hand. It was a big house in the Victorian style. We took vacations all over Europe, lived materially luxurious lives. But I didn't feel rich. I still felt like an orphan.

I don't think my father has the ability to empathize. He likes for people to mind their own business, and he likes to mind his. He likes fixable things with obvious rules. My parents' relationship was hopelessly broken, and it had no rules. *All's fair in love and war* and all that. We lived in the big house about two years. It felt like the most stable time of my childhood.

The first and only time I ever saw my father cry was in this house. He had just gotten a phone call from Iraq. His mother was dead. One of his brothers, an Iraqi soldier, had died earlier that year.

The lights were off and daylight from the big bay window at the head of the dining room cut through the gloom, transfixing the dust particles in the air. My father stood in front of the window holding himself up with his left hand on the back of his usual chair, his arm straight and stiff. I rarely saw my father so still. He was a mover. My mother was the sitter. He didn't take his eyes off the window, some distant point, as I approached quietly. I saw the nearly dry tracks of recent tears on his cheeks under his far-off eyes. I could see through them for once. I could see grief and longing. It glimmered there nakedly for a moment until he registered my presence. His faced closed then like the doors to a secret society in which I had no membership.

"What's wrong, Dad?"

"Nothing, bab. I'm okay."

I looked into his eyes waiting for them to open up to me again. Nothing.

"I'm fine, bab. Really."

He looked away again. I walked out of the room. I started to tear up. Both for what I had seen in his eyes, and for the fact that he had closed it off from me again. From us.

I came into the living room to find my mother, usually the sitter, pacing around, plucking knickknacks and books from one table and moving them to others, full of nervous energy. There were half-finished cigarettes smoking in at least two ashtrays. She was talking to herself quietly until I entered the room. She replied to the question my face was asking: *What is wrong with Dad?* But she wasn't really talking to me. She was still talking to herself aloud, as she often did.

"Maybe now he knows how it feels. How I felt…"

He hadn't been there for her when *her* mother died. Now it was his turn. No wonder he was closed off.

We lived in the big house for maybe another year after that. But it couldn't last. Finally, Dad moved to Poulton-le-fylde, fifty miles away. He took me with him, leaving Troy and Layla with my mother in the big house. He moved in with another woman, Lorraine. He had finally conceded the Great Argument. My mother had finally won. Whatever that meant.

Every time my father left, my mother took it out on me. This last time was the worst. I blamed her for his absence, and I blamed her for our misery. I started to tell her what I thought, but she wouldn't hear it. She immediately turned the argument on me, but unlike most times, when I capitulated in silence and let her say her fill, this time I talked back to her. So she resorted to violence. We were in the kitchen, and she grabbed the nearest instrument—a big metal stirring spoon. I turned to run. She caught up with me and hit me in the back, knocking me to the ground. I had had enough.

My grandfather, my mother's father lived a few miles away. I walked to his house. He came to the door. I explained the situation. I showed him the welt on my back, the size of my face. He got on the phone with my mother.

"Akeela's here, Sheree. She's going to stay with me for a while."

I loved my grandfather. Out of fourteen grandchildren, I was his favorite. I respected him. He had a thick Scottish accent, and he smelled very bad—like urine and wet dog. The other kids used to make fun of him, mocking his Scottish accent and scrunching up their noses when he was around. They didn't care if he heard or saw it. But I didn't care how he smelled. I liked his accent. He was quiet and sweet—dependable and consistent.

He had already planned a trip to Spain for that following week, so he decided to take me with him. My father came over the day before we left with some money. My grandfather met him at the door:

"Here's some money for the trip. For Akeela. I'm going to talk to Lorraine. When you all get back, Akeela can come live with us."

We went to Benalmaderna, Costa Del Sol. *The coast of the sun.* It lived up to its name. I spent most days at the beach. I talked to boys. I made friends. It was easier for me to get along with boys. They made more sense to me. Girls my age always seemed to be competing with me for a prize I didn't know about. They made me small to make themselves great, and I didn't like these games. My grandfather took me to dinner at night. He would walk with me, linking arms, escorting me like I was a fine lady at court. When we talked, even about trivial things, he always made me feel like he was wholly there. His mind was not elsewhere thinking about important adult things. He was focused on our conversation, the most important thing in the world to him right then. That magical trip had to end. And when it did, my father took me with him to Poulton-le-fylde to live at his girlfriend's house.

MY DAD'S OTHER WOMAN LORRAINE was well-spoken around my father. Didn't curse like my mother, always exuding propriety and class. After his first failed marriage, my father was looking for a different kind of woman, a different kind of business venture.

Other than her show of classiness though, I never saw anything in Lorraine to warrant male attention. She really was *ugly*. All around. She had jaundiced eyes, splotchy skin, a large, hooked nose, and a rotund flat-chested pear-body that she stuffed into jeans like too much filling in a sausage skin. And her looks were the best part about her. She was a calculating, hateful, manipulative harpy. The only thing she needed to complete the perfect picture of a storybook witch was a black dress and a besom broom. And she smelled like Limburger cheese—that awful yeasty toe jam smell. Altogether a hideous person. And a chain-smoking drunk.

She had a daughter, Melissa, her understudy in petty nastiness. They never used my name, calling me "it" instead.

"Would it please pass the butter? Really, I've been waiting quite long enough. Oh, dear… Would it *please* not use the butter knife to butter its bread. Use *its own* knife. Hasn't it learned *any* manners?"

Lorraine would spill things on me regularly. I knew it was on purpose. We would be at dinner, my father sitting across from me, Lorraine at the head (it was *her* house after all). She would look me in the eye and pour her wine into my lap while my father wasn't looking. "Oh, dear me. You are so very clumsy." My father never noticed. She made it seem like I was a hopeless cretin that she took pity on for my father's sake. He never challenged this.

Lorraine was drinking all the time. Boxed red wine. My room was right next to the kitchen where she spent a lot of her time, so she stocked my room with snacks so I'd have no reason to venture out. One time, I needed to iron my skirt. The board and the iron were in the kitchen. She sat there at the table watching me, her eyes tracking me through a squint. Her arms were half-folded, one forearm straight up, a prop for that ubiquitous cigarette, the glass of red wine on the round table in front of her.

Later, she said to my father, "Why don't you buy Akeela her own iron?"

My father looked at me like, "See, she *does* care about you."

He didn't realize that he had married a much less attractive version of my mother who was just a little bit better at hiding her feelings. My dad was fine with that. As long as she minded her business, he didn't need to know what she really felt. Or what she did when he wasn't there.

My father didn't enroll me in school in Poulton. Instead, I spent most of my out-of-room time working at Lorraine's face-painting booth at Pleasure Beach, Blackpool's amusement park. Blackpool was a resort town on the coast of the Irish Sea. It was about six miles from Lorraine's.

I spent a lot of time getting comfortable in my own skin. I had some shelter from the world in my room. I was still finding out who I was. I knew I didn't want to end up like my mother. But I didn't even know who my father was. Where did he come from? His reticence made me even more curious.

I worked the booth in Blackpool with Lorraine's sisters. Even though Lorraine owned it, she was never there. Her sisters all disliked her too; I think they may have even stolen money from her. Lorraine had a similar relationship with them that my mother had with her sisters: jealous and competitive. But they were permissive and gentle with me. Reminded me a little of Angela.

If I haven't mentioned my aunt Angela yet, it's because she doesn't really fit in this story. She sticks out in it like a rosebush in a cemetery. Angela was my mother's younger sister, the youngest child of six. I think Angela was Nana's favorite. She was "the pretty one." My mother hated her for this. My father even tried to get with Angela once. I was so afraid his attentions would scare her off. Or worse, that she would accept his affections: that the part of my life I could hardly endure would swallow up the only part that kept me going.

I had complicated emotions toward Angela. I wanted so badly for her to be my mother. Almost all of my pleasant childhood memories involve her. Or her father. But I also wanted to protect her from me, from my life, my family. She lived nearby throughout my childhood; she always seemed to be close. A feeling of her nearness was often all I needed to cope. If things got too bad, Angela was always just down the road. I think she may have been the one who told my dad we were with the Shepherds.

Angela got her personality from her father. I don't have many memories of him aside from my time living at his house or our trip to Spain. He was a docile man, a tea drinker and a TV watcher. Always a gentleman. He was like that quiet estuary in the mountains that you find out later is the source of a huge and mighty river. Angela was the river.

The times I spent with Angela, just her and me, were the sweetest times of my youth. She took me with her shopping or on the town. She liked to splurge. Maybe she was a bit vain, a bit materialistic, a bit insecure. But to me, she was all energy and sunshine, everything I wanted to be—smart, sophisticated, and tender. She was snarky without being mean. People loved her. Strangers paid attention while she was around.

Her apartment was a haven for me. It was always neat and orderly. Her bed was always made. It even had the decorative cushions on it which she would carefully organize on a love seat before she went to bed.

But she wasn't controlling. I could jump on her bed. Play dress up with her clothes. She had a huge two-piece L-shaped dresser, white painted wood with gold handles and trim. Full of clothes. She changed her appearance often—her clothes, hair color, accessories—always just ahead of the latest trends. I wouldn't have been surprised to find out that she had been the one setting them. She helped me put on makeup. She made sure I had deodorant. A bra and tampons when I was old enough. I could talk to her about anything.

I couldn't talk to my parents about *anything*. I hid my life and my real feelings from them. I remember the few times I complained to my dad about how Lorraine treated me. He wouldn't hear it.

"Lorraine's good to you. You're being just like your mother."

But Angela would listen. She would never accuse. Sometimes she said very little. She understood the value of a friendly silence.

I remember times with her in snatches. The moments seem trivial in their circumstances, but I know I remember them so vividly because of how good I felt then. Free. Like riding in the top level of an orange and brown double-decker bus, something I never did (my father and mother drove us everywhere). Angela gave me the window seat, and I remember looking down on the passing pedestrians and storefronts with a sense of wholeness and security. Angela bought me a Raggedy Ann Doll and a candy bar for my sixth birthday. It's funny. Nana bought me something just like that for my birthday every year. But it didn't mean anything to me. I kept Angela's doll with me everywhere I went. Maybe I was a little old for dolls. I had aged lop-sided though. In many ways, I was a very little girl until my teenage years. Yet I had heard, seen, and endured things that most adults have never imagined.

She knew the situation with my parents. She allowed me to live a child's life. She felt sorry for me, but she didn't show it too often. I felt unburdened with her. And if I caught her looking at me very occasionally with her eyelids weighed down at the corners with concern and pity, she would quickly brighten up and move things along. How I wished she were my mother.

ANYWAY, LORRAINE'S SISTERS REMINDED ME of Angela a bit. They were motherly like her. It seemed most any woman in the world would make a better mother than the ones I got. My mother. Mrs. Shepherd. Now Lorraine. Was it me? Did I deserve this? Did I make them like this?

Lorraine always asked about my mother. "What does your mother look like?" Lorraine's attempts to look good were comical. The bleach she applied to her hair made it thin and frizzy, and her brown roots still showed anyway. She tried to fatten up her thin lips by surrounding them with lipstick and puckering them constantly. She also sucked in her cheeks, and her cheekbones were already too prominent. Maybe she thought that was pretty. So she accentuated them further with badly blended bruise red blush. Her face looked like it belonged to a hooker clownfish. I would have even felt bad for her if she hadn't been so mean.

Whenever I rode alone with her in the car, she drove like Cruella de Vil, with the same cackling laugh. I think it was just to scare me. She would look over at me for longer than was safe with wide yellow eyes. She was probably drunk. I wasn't afraid of her though. She was a pathetic person. Whenever she asked me about my mother, I guess she wanted me to say something mean. Something that would make her feel superior. Those same schoolgirl games. *Mirror, mirror, in the passenger seat... who is fairer, me or Sheree?*

So I guess I did have a fairy tale childhood. Complete with ogres, witches, sullen kings, wicked step-mothers, maidens locked up in various prisons... secluded from the world. I was Rapunzel with my long hair. Or Sleeping Beauty. All the boys thought I was frigid as a corpse, maybe a lesbian. I couldn't help it. I wasn't allowed to talk to them. The only thing missing from my storybook life was the happy ending. You know, the part where Prince Charming storms in on a white horse and rescues me.

LAYLA VISITED ME IN POULTON. She asked when I was coming home. I guess she meant to mom's. She looked up to me in some ways. She had been a nuisance to me growing up, as younger siblings often are. If I was invited to a party or anything, my mom would always say, "Take Layla, or you're not going." I resented Layla for this, which is what my mother wanted. It seemed she was dedicated to making sure my relationship with Layla mirrored her relationship with Angela. Which was strange because, in that scenario, Layla would have been Angela. Which meant *I* was *my mother.*

Nonetheless, Layla went with me most everywhere. We shared a room for most of my life. She snored. She was messy. Of course I had to pick up after her. I had no privacy with Layla. And she acted the brat often, tag-teaming with Troy against me. Troy always excused Mom for her behavior, blaming me when things at the house were tense. Layla. Troy. Mom. No, I wasn't coming home.

I wanted badly to escape. I did nothing but work in Blackpool or brood in my room. One day, I found one of my father's tapes: an album by an Egyptian singer, Amr Diab. I had a boom box in my room, a gift from my father, and I listened to that album over and over again. I understood none of the Arabic lyrics, but they were sung so sweetly, every phrase lilting and pleading, like the melody couldn't contain the singer's feeling which spilled out on either side of it. One time, my father showed up at my door, surprised to hear the sound. And delighted.

"You really like this?"

"Yeah. It's pretty cool. Will you tell me what he's saying?"

My dad sat with me for a while then, struggling to translate.

"*Matkhafeesh*... uhhh... Don't be afraid... I will not have forgotten you... It is not important who calls for me... I cannot live without your eyes... Your eyes... Your eyes... I can't live without another love... Another... Another... Another..."

After that, he started to take more of an interest in me. I was fourteen and this was the first time my father had spent any real quality time with me. It was intoxicating. Maybe this is who I was.

He started to talk to me about his homeland, those embellished memories that had accrued fantastical dimensions in his mind. But I believed them. After all, Amr Diab was very attractive. I began to think that maybe the Arabs that made it over here were the worst of the bunch. That things were different over there.

I talked to my dad's father, Hayder, for the first time around that time. He called from Iraq, and my father was very excited about the interest I had taken in his heritage. My grandfather talked to me briefly, told me he would send me some more tapes. My father got back on the phone, and started rattling things off in Arabic: that same harsh sound I had heard before when my dad's friends came over—like battling coffee grinders.

And then one day, rather suddenly, my father asked me in passing whether I might want to visit Iraq sometime.

"Sure, Dad. That's sounds like it could be fun."

"Great. Great. I'm so glad you feel that way. Listen, I'm done with Lorraine. I just can't take it any more. I know you've never liked her anyway. Look, things are going to get pretty crazy around here for a while until I find a new place for us to live in. So, it would be easier if you weren't here to have to deal with it. It'll take me two weeks to get everything in order. Tops."

"So what are you saying?"

"You'll go to Iraq."

"Now?"

"Yeah. You just told me you wanted to go. What's the matter with you? You'll see my family. See a little more of the world. It'll be great, bab."

I didn't want to upset him, and I could see in his eyes that he expected me to be happy. Besides, I had wanted to leave this life behind. I was too stubborn to go back to my mom's. Things with my dad wouldn't have even been that bad, if it weren't for Cruella de Vil and my wicked step-sisters. I was ready for something new, and maybe my father's homeland was really my homeland too.

Just a couple of weeks later, I was ready to go. He had already bought me a plane ticket. He had it all worked out. I would stay with my grandfather. He would send for me when he was ready. I didn't argue.

We couldn't tell my mother where I was going. She had warned me about Iraq many times.

"No matter what your father says, don't you ever go to Iraq, Akeela. They'll kill you. They're all just like your father. Only worse."

I had no reason to believe her. I didn't know what to think. I was just ready to leave. To taste something new. Anything.

My dad told me to write mom a letter saying I was going to Switzerland for a skiing trip. I didn't tell Angela. My dad said there was no reason to worry anyone. That it was just for a little while. That I'd be back before anyone noticed.

THE DAY I LEFT, MY father drove me to the London airport in his white work van—about a six hour drive. I had never experienced my father like this, attentive and kind. I had longed for this attention for so long. Why did I have to leave *now*? Just a few weeks after he had started taking a real human interest in me, he was sending me off… But just for a little while. A couple weeks. I could do this. For him.

When we parked at the airport, I started to get out of the car. My dad told me to wait. He took the Rolex off of his wrist.

"Give this to your grandfather." Then he took a huge roll of bills from his pocket. "And this."

I put the money into my pocket. I kept checking it every few minutes, patting my jeans. It made me very nervous to have that much money on me.

Up to this point in the trip, my father had been very excited about me going to Iraq, almost like he was jealous that I was going rather than him. "It's going to be great," he would say with a smile and a slight shake of the head. But right before I left him at the check-in gate, his demeanor changed. He seemed hesitant. Guilty.

"Are you sure you really want to go?"

"Yes, Dad. I told you."

"I know, bab… I know. It's just. You never really showed any interest before. I want to make sure… this is… for you."

He wanted *me* to put *his* mind at ease? I was the one about to travel to some distant desert kingdom. Why was he so concerned? I felt a loyalty to him at that moment that I had never felt before, so I said what I thought he needed to hear.

"No, Dad. I'm fine. I'll be all right. Right? It's just for a little while. You'll get things sorted, and I'll be back before you know it."

"Okay." He paused still unsure, like he was calculating something in his head. "Yeah. Yes. Well. Goodbye. Please help your grandfather. Take care of him."

I touched the lump in my pocket. *Still there.* Then my father embraced me. A real fatherly hug. I had waited my whole life to feel this. Why did it take these circumstances for him to finally talk to me—for him to finally love me? The hug had a finality to it, like the tenderness of a eulogy.

You know when you are a kid and you want a piece of candy or something, and you fixate on it until you believe that touching it to your lips will be the consummation of your childhood existence? But then you get it after all that and… it's just a piece of candy. Longing for it was more significant than getting it. That's kind of how I felt about my father's affection. I just couldn't trust it. I wanted to so badly, but there was something not quite right about it. I didn't even know if it would still be there when I returned.

I turned to leave him. An Arab flight attendant, my escort, hurried me to the departure gate, her hips churning ahead of me in her navy blue skirt. She waited almost long enough for me to catch up before she continued. She was a busy woman. I looked at her as I approached. She had a face like an expertly cut gemstone. Milk chocolate skin and silky straight black hair. A beautiful, westernized Arab. Would I look like this when I returned?

We were approaching some metal double doors ahead. I turned to look for my father. He was still waiting there at the check-in gate. I could see him between the other passengers as they weaved around each other on their different courses—his silent hand waving goodbye. He already had his sunglasses on, his aviators. I couldn't see his eyes anymore. The flight attendant called to me. I walked through the gray-brown double doors, which closed behind me with a click. And he was gone.

"Don't be afraid of people, who can kill the body but cannot kill the soul. The only one you should fear is the one who can destroy the soul and the body in hell."

Matthew 10:28

II: An Iraqi Woman

WHEN THE FLIGHT ATTENDANT DROPPED me off at the departure gate, she looked me up and down, and raised one corner of her hard mouth and both shoulders in an almost imperceptible shrug as if to say, "Well, it is what it is. Good luck. You're going to need it."

Other passengers had already congregated about the gate, some of them in traditional Arabic dress. They stood out like sunspots—their black robes and hoods against the neon brightness of London and her people. I had my hair down with gold hoops in my ears. I wore a long-sleeved topaz shirt and stone washed jeans. I probably could have passed for eighteen or twenty. I was not yet fifteen.

On the plane, which was bound for Amman, Jordan, I sat next to a cheerful and cheeky Jordanian man who took the window seat without thinking about it. He talked with great enthusiasm about returning home, about all the money he would make off of the outdated electronic gadgets he had accumulated in London on the cheap. He unzipped his carry-on to show me all his old Walkmans and pagers, picking some of them up and turning them in the light like jewels. After talking about himself and his sunny prospects in Jordan for quite some time, he finally asked me why I was going to Jordan. He didn't seem all that interested, using his pause in speech to take a gulp of his drink.

"I'm actually going to Iraq." He spit out his drink like his mouth was an atomizer, his enthusiasm immediately shriveling. His smile transformed instantly into a scowl.

"Why would you want to do that? No. No. You stay in Jordan. Much better. There is nothing in Iraq."

My already delicate peace concerning the trip was eroding. The flight attendants looked at me with concern, tending to me like I was a terminal patient, whispering to one another together, shaking their heads, pointing at me furtively.

When our in-flight meal came, my Jordanian plane mate threw his salt and pepper packets at me with a dark chuckle.

"Here. You'll need these where you're going."

He didn't talk to me much after that, leaning his head against the cabin wall, staring at the clouds through the tiny portal window. It was like I was an offense to him. Was this trip really that much of a mistake? My father had talked it up enough. But then his guilty look. The flight attendants. This Jordanian. What did they all know that they weren't telling me?

WHEN WE FINALLY LANDED IN Jordan, the Amman airport was my first introduction to just how alien this place was. In Britain, the passengers had lined up quietly in orderly queues. Even the anarchist punks with their fiery red and black mohawks had stood patiently in line like everyone else, another well-oiled cog in a grand machine. I had not stood out there.

On the other hand, Amman International Airport was a cageless, mute-colored zoo. Dirty and dark, the majority of the people here wore black and dirty white. People camped out in the middle of thoroughfares, sat on the floor wherever they wanted. There weren't lines. There was a human dough ball of line cutters and jostlers, ceaselessly kneaded, folding over onto itself in an endless game of king of the mud heap. If people weren't bumping into me wordlessly, they were staring at me—at my green eyes, my uncovered hair—wagging their heads.

My grandfather materialized, grabbed my hand, and started leading me out of the madness. He said nothing to me. No hello. Nothing. Whenever anyone looked at him with me, he said the same two words in Arabic, and kept moving. I found out later what he was saying—"Son's daughter." People stopped and gawked at us, this green-eyed Westerner being led about by this gray-haired Muslim.

We reached the baggage carousel. I tried to grab my own bags as they passed. My grandfather stopped me, anger showing briefly on his face.

"No. You are woman now."

He pulled the bags off, and pulled me out of the airport in much the same way, like I was a suitcase with legs instead of wheels. We came outside, and I got my first look at Amman. It looked a little like my father's descriptions: a fine city in the hills with whitewashed square buildings sometimes dwarfed by larger steel and glass structures. It was a city in the middle of two places—a Muslim city touched by the West. It reminded me of the flight attendant. Spare and hard, but beautiful enough. I didn't yet feel that far from home. This place had smog too. I never thought I would be comforted to see smog hugging the horizon.

My father had booked a hotel for us to stay the night. We took a taxi to the hotel, and it wasn't until we were sitting in the back of it with my stuff packed in the trunk that my grandfather finally settled a little and faced me, studying me a bit formally.

"You look like your father. Green eyes. Very good here." He pointed to his eyes and nodded, like maybe I hadn't understood what he was saying.

"Thanks," is all I could say.

He spit some instructions at the cab driver in Arabic. I felt the money in my pocket again.

"My dad told me to give you this." As soon as he saw the money, he brought his body close to it, keeping his hands near his stomach, blocking the thick roll from view with his torso, enveloping it with his body as much as with his hands. He pushed it into his pants and looked sideways at the driver to ascertain what he had seen.

I was more careful giving him the Rolex, imitating my grandfather's carefulness and passing it to him below the driver's line of vision. He wasn't concerned about the watch as much. He put it on directly. He even showed it to the cab driver proudly, and said something in Arabic that felt like it meant, "Look at what my lovely granddaughter brought me." I thought about how little I really knew or understood of their ways.

The driver stopped in front of a big white concrete cube of a building. Most of the city was white: painted concrete, mortar, or adobe. Dust filled the air and stuck to everyone's clothes in a fine layer. The air was dry and empty and the sunlight had nowhere to bury itself in the day. It just ricocheted around and stung your skin and eyes.

When we got to the hotel, my grandfather said he had to go for a bit, that he would be right back. When he returned, he had ice cream cones and two sweating glass bottles of Coca-Cola.

"Coca-Cola?" I waved my hand and shook my head. He held it out to me still and steady, like it was the last one I would ever see. I took it and the ice cream, working on them slowly—too anxious to feel like eating or drinking. He ate the ice cream with his teeth, biting into it like he hadn't eaten in days.

That afternoon we met a Jordanian friend of his who had brought his son, Ali, who asked my grandfather if he could escort me around Amman to show me the sights. My grandfather complied. Amman has a rich history. The line jostling at the airport was a microcosm of its past. Rome had conquered this place once, as had various other kings. Each conqueror left behind the relics of his rule—bits of architecture or language—like he was trying in vain to hold his place in line. His place in time. Ali walked me through a Roman amphitheater, telling me how old it was. I forgot most of what he said. His English was good. He was handsome. It seemed strange that one of the first times I had been alone with a man other than a relative should be *here*. Amman is beautiful at night. The lights are few, most of them yellow and amber. You can see almost all of the stars still. You can feel the day's sunlight vibrating in the ground and the walls at night, all the surfaces still warm as a pizza stone. I felt much better after my visit with Ali. Hopeful.

The next day, we would make our way to Iraq. Jordan lies on the east border of Israel. It has an odd shape, like a robed and hooded Arab woman facing a hard wind coming from the West, blowing her scarf out behind her. We would drive through the middle of that scarf, over the Syrian desert, crossing the border into Iraq through a short strip of desert it shares with Jordan at the tip of the scarf.

When I awoke, my grandfather was already awake. He had our things piled together on the floor. He was pacing a bit. Nervous. When he saw I was awake, he stopped pacing, put both of his feet together and clasped his hands. He didn't speak English well, and it brought out a certain delicacy in him that was undetectable when he spoke Arabic.

"Okay. First. Don't be afraid." *Don't be afraid.* He could have said that in Arabic—*Matkhafeesh.* I could hear Amr Diab singing it.

"Long, long way. Many soldiers. Police. No look!" He wagged

his finger and modeled what I should do, walking in place with his head down, eyes to the floor.

"No cowboy." He pointed to my jeans which I had worn to bed, then gestured to a black thing draped on his bed. He used two hands with his palms upright, like Vanna White or something. I took the long-sleeved black dress to the bathroom and put it on. When I came out, my grandfather looked at my hair.

"No hair." He helped me put on the hood, a hijab, making sure to cover every curly black strand. I looked in the mirror. Aside from my green eyes, I looked like I could pass for a regular Arab girl, but this still felt like dress up. None of it felt real to me yet. My grandfather looked me over.

"Very good."

Once in the cab, my grandfather told the driver where we were going: Baghdad. The driver turned. *That sure is a long way* was written on his face, though I have no idea what he said. My grandfather gave him the money up front, which immediately put him in a good mood. They acted like old friends almost immediately.

Most of the cars I saw in the Middle East were old model Toyotas, most of them white at one time. This cab was no different aside from its bright yellow paint, sand-matted and rusty in spots. Once we got outside of Amman, the roads were not well-maintained. The car bounced and creaked, kicking up dust clouds, but still sputtering on. My grandfather and the driver talked in Arabic. I looked out the window for a while. Little to see. This desert didn't even have dunes. Flat white stretches with an occasional rock would dissolve into the horizon—the edge of the world evaporating into the sky. The road in front of us cut through the bright bleakness like an obsidian serpent, white in the distance until it too shimmered and hesitated into swirls of cream and baby blue, like heat would melt and stir it all together eventually.

Then a blurry black dot appeared in the distance like a gnat on a lens. As we drew closer, shapes started to resolve—a sort of low flat-roofed hut with four men standing beside it. It was our first checkpoint.

The four soldiers all looked identical to me from the glimpse I got. I remembered almost too late that I was not supposed to be looking at anyone. They wore flat hats, and carried long rifles. Every one of them had a clean, trimmed mustache on his sun beaten face. They were yelling in Arabic as they stopped the car. We had to get out. They pulled everything out of the car. They searched everywhere in the car, pulling up floor mats and even searching under the spare tire. The whole process took about twenty or thirty minutes. While three of them scoured the cab, one of them asked my grandfather questions in Arabic. My grandfather looked extremely agitated and nervous, sweat rolling off his nose.

When we got back in the cab, I asked my grandfather what they were looking for.

"Soap, shampoo. Black market to smuggle."

Soap and shampoo? Forget the war on drugs. These people were waging a war on personal hygiene. And from the looks of it, they were winning.

We were stopped about six or so times, but the stop at the border was the most extensive. This time, they brought me and my grandfather into a bare office of sorts—with a desk and a metal chair on wheels. A sharp-eyed officer sat in the chair looking like the template from which they had cloned all of his junior officers. I caught barely a glimpse of him before I put my head back down. It was excruciating. *Why can't I look around?*

What are they afraid of?

I couldn't tell if these men were soldiers or police. It was always hard to tell the difference in the Middle East. The main officer spoke a little English, with a thick accent:

"Why are you here?"

I continued to look at the ground.

"Hello? I *talk* to you."

He was talking to *me?* My grandfather said something in Arabic. I had heard it many times before: "Son's daughter." He continued on in Arabic, but the main officer interrupted.

"You for news? Reporter?"

I pretended I didn't know what was going on. I could feel my heart punching my rib cage. All I saw was this small patch of concrete, blurring at the edges from the sweat that kept dripping into my downturned eyes. It's amazing how much interest you can find in even the most mundane thing if you stop to focus on it for a while. I thought about what tools they had used to pour and level this concrete. I could see the swirls of it, the faint streaks of yellow brown that had been mixed into it, dust trapped inside it and laying on it with boot prints and bare swaths from shuffling feet or nervous sitters, pebbles here and there with stepping stone pock marks trailing behind them in the dust, tracking the path they had taken from the toe of someone on important government business.

My grandfather spoke again for a while. Finally, he convinced the officer I was not a news reporter, and they let us go, saying something to my grandfather that sounded like a warning.

Any time the cab had to stop at a checkpoint, my grandfather and the driver acted like guilty children, scared and compliant. But when we pulled back out into the open desert again, their demeanor changed completely. They would get indignant, with their hands waving in the air. Their heads would bob in agreement while each delivered his version of the grand effrontery they had just endured. I didn't understand what they were saying, but in my head, it sounded something like,

"Who did those guys think they were? Asking *me* what I was doing there? What does it look like I'm doing. I'm driving a cab, idiot."

"I know. I know. Man, if they had pressed me just a little bit harder, I would have snapped. I don't know what I would have done to them. But let's just say it wouldn't have been pretty, I can tell you that!"

Distant from the threat, they resumed an easy bravado and boldness, making forceful and probably foul gestures with their arms and hands, laughing together. After the cab driver had given in to a particularly long and hardy laughing fit, my grandfather turned to me and introduced me to his favorite English word. He twirled his finger around in the air like it was a horizontal flag: "Crazy." It was a fitting word for the place.

After driving all morning and all day, we finally made it into the heart of Iraq: Baghdad, the capital city.

BAGHDAD LOOKED EVEN LESS LIKE the pictures my father had painted than Amman had. It was further removed from all the things I knew, and less evenly amalgamated—it was a schizophrenic city. A few shiny black Mercedes with opaquely tinted windows joined the population of dented Toyotas, all mulling down a cobbly street with an abandoned window-smashed car chassis to the side of it. A brass-gated Spanish villa with a red-orange tiled roof and a black and white checkered driveway stood like a guarded military compound next to a run-down mud-brick hovel. I had never seen such poverty and such affluence stuck together without any admixture. Baghdad had no middle class.

We pulled up to a decent looking one-story house and were greeted outside by an older woman, my Aunt Selma, and her three daughters. They were wealthy by Iraqi standards, and their house had many of the English luxuries I had up to that point considered certainties of civilization.

My grandfather pulled our luggage out of the trunk of the cab and said a final warm goodbye to his freshly minted old friend, the cab driver, whom he would probably never see again. My grandfather was exhausted from the travel and the stress. As soon as we had gotten settled inside, he went to his room and fell asleep. We would leave again the following morning.

I wasn't hungry at dinner. I had eaten almost nothing since arriving in Jordan, but I had no appetite. My stomach had filled up with the stone soup of the unknowns that awaited me.

My Great Aunt Selma was my grandmother's sister, a portly, quiet woman and a devout Muslim. Her oldest daughter had just moved back in after her divorce from a respected Baghdad politician. She had bleached blonde hair and a snobbish air. I got the feeling my aunt was a little ashamed of her. Aunt Selma's husband wore a goatee and drove a Cadillac; he had little presence at the house, remaining entirely aloof while I was there. It felt like a woman's house, cluttered with their voices and their tastes. I woke many times in the night sweating. What had I gotten myself into?

The next morning, Selma drove us to a bus station. We didn't talk. She spent the whole time praying in Arabic, I don't think she was used to driving and it scared her. It would have scared me too. No one seemed to follow any road rules, if there were any, passing each other even on busy streets, pulling into traffic without signalling. A mob, a mechanized version of the airport — the same complete disregard for manners and common courtesy. They drove like they were just walking together in a big crowd; like the metal of the cars that surrounded them didn't even exist.

But there were other conventions, ones alien to me, that no one dared break. Women did not make eye contact with men. They did not walk the streets alone, always trailing some distance behind their male escorts with their eyes averted. In Baghdad, I saw women in full orthodox Muslim dress for the first time, robed in black from head to toe. They looked like black-cloth KKK members, completely shrouded, with even their eyes covered. Some of them had their eyes even further obscured by an extra layer of mesh, their hoods pinned tightly under their chins. I learned later that colored eyes required this extra screen, since they were so prized.

For all the yelling and haggling and jostling that went on in the chaotic streets, there was the presence of this invisible iron hand, an oppressive force that moved people into their proper places, so that no one had to think about anything or anyone else. The iron hand aligned everything automatically, presenting each person with the lot appropriate to his station. The air was choked with it, much stuffier than Jordan. Much scarier.

We came to our bus, a rusty Vanagon with rails installed on the roof for baggage, among which was a wire cage containing two clucking chickens. We said a short goodbye to Selma, who was anxious to get back home—to complete this trip.

Our bus driver may have been drunk. He drove like it. The inside of the bus was filthy, like a public bathroom at a train station. The bus lurched forward and we were on our way to Basra, a distance of over three hundred miles. The rural roads in Iraq were worse than in Jordan, filled with pits, crumbling away at the edges. They smelled like sulfur. There was barely one usable lane no matter how you sliced it, but cars didn't slow down or yield for oncoming traffic. It seemed miraculous that we didn't get in an accident. We finally pulled into a station at Basra where we got a cab to complete our journey.

Civilization, the West, had been peeling off layer by layer since I had landed in Jordan. I had been shocked a little by the Amman airport. Baghdad had been even further removed. But nothing had prepared me for rural Iraq.

I had taken England for granted growing up. I hadn't thought much about other places, but I figured they got along much the same way we did. But now I realized just how different a place I had come to. Things in rural Basra were bleak. Some houses were made of dirt or mud bricks, and even the concrete houses looked like they would soon return to dirt. It was creeping up the sides of everything, like the dust held the note of debt on this place and was about to foreclose. Most houses didn't have windows, just holes roughly cut into the sides, some of them covered with frayed and color-bled rugs, others slatted with end-spiked bars.

After all this traveling, I was caked in sweat and dust, stiff in my joints, parched, with a stone in my stomach. I was ready to get to my grandfather's house, take a shower, and crash.

When we drove into my grandfather's neighborhood, I saw a crowd of people had gathered. I wondered what this was all about. Then I noticed they were all pointing at the car, and a noise erupted from them like nothing I had ever heard before. It was like a Cherokee war yelp, a rebel yell, from every mouth at once. It startled me. I thought something had gone terribly wrong. Maybe they were going to drag me out of this car, tie my hands and feet to the ends of a pole and carry me upside down to some headhunters' feast. Turns out they were just happy to see me. Raising this holy racket was their way of saying so, but I really wasn't in the mood. Shy by nature, in this increasingly alien place, I wanted some peace and quiet. I wasn't going to get it.

My grandfather led me up to the entrance of his house. About a dozen people lived there and they all stood outside to greet us. I got the grand tour from an aunt. When we walked through the door, which had a floral lattice screen of black wrought iron, we entered into… the kitchen. It reminded me of a rustic version of a hospital kitchen. Bare. No decorations. A wooden table sat in the center with no chairs. A black kettle rested on the stove top. A big room with basically nothing in it.

We walked through the kitchen. None of the doorways to the main living areas had doors, just openings. Adjacent to the kitchen was a washroom with a tiled floor and a drain. Buckets, cans, and basins lined the walls in stacks. Huge bars of green soap stuck to a low shelf. This was the rationed soap, the only legal kind in Iraq.

Next I saw my grandfather's room. He had a fine bedroom set, all handmade—a big bed with a matching armoire beside it, a dresser, and a lamp table. He kept the armoire locked. It was stocked full of black market goods: scented French soap, aftershave, shampoo, medicines of all kinds, and his favorite cologne—Drakkar Noir.

Past his room was the formal dining room. I don't think they ever ate there. It had a Western appearance with a table and chairs, a formal service with silverware, a sofa on one side, and another freezer, the only thing in the room that saw any use. Everything else looked like it had been set up once long ago, and time had managed to dishevel it only slightly, draping it all in an even sheet of dust, like the surviving possessions of a dead man's estate.

I had stepped back in time. The newest fixtures in the house were fifteen years old. The next room, the family room, had a few mismatched sofas and chairs arranged in a lopsided circle around a TV—a wood-encased living fossil. This TV could have projected the premiere of *Leave It To Beaver*.

A picture of a man in military dress hung on the wall of the living room. My aunt, the tour guide, paused in front of it before moving on. I found out later that it was Hussein, my father's brother. He had died in the Iraq-Iran War, leaving behind this woman and her two sons. They all stayed with my grandfather. My father felt it his duty to care for them, his dead brother's family.

The next room was the largest in the house, with low bench seating around three quarters of it. The main entryway with the house's only phone led into this big entertaining parlor, and I imagined it was where the family received guests. Letting me enter through the kitchen was a sign that they considered me family already... that they weren't standing on ceremony with me. The entertainment room boasted a traditional Persian style rug in the center of it, threadbare and filthy. Nothing in the house had escaped dirt or dust. It was in or on everything, regularly reminding them all, "Remember that I own everything here. Don't get too comfortable."

There were four bedrooms and a bathroom upstairs. The house was very large by Iraqi standards and had been added on to. My widow aunt lived in one room with her two sons. She was a quiet woman who minded her own business, obeying my grandfather without a word, following the iron hand without any friction. She was a perfect Muslim woman. Anything that made her unique had been erased by years of automatic ritual and interminable domesticity. Perhaps that's why I can't remember her name.

My uncle Ahmed lived in another room upstairs with his wife and son. He had green eyes like my dad. His snooty wife looked down on me, laughing at my social foibles and mispronunciations of Arabic.

Laith, another uncle, lived with his wife and newborn boy in the third bedroom. They had bandaged up their baby from head to toe. He looked like an infant mummy. They told me this was an old Muslim custom, that it ensured good posture later in life. The baby didn't seem to like it though. He cried all the time.

They had prepared the fourth bedroom for me. It had been my dad's oldest brother Mafheed's room, but he stayed in the family room for now. He had moved back in with my grandfather after divorcing his wife. He had left her and two kids in Baghdad.

My room had a twin bed, a bookshelf, a dresser, and a window, which, like most windows, had spiked iron bars outside it. I got a fridge later from Mafheed. He would stock it with candy and soda—black market goods.

The most striking feature of my room was a painting that hung on the wall opposite the head of my bed, so I could lie down and stare at it if I wanted. The painting, in a well-executed surrealistic style, depicted a bald, muscular man, shirtless, reaching up to grasp the upturned bow of a capsized boat, half-sunk already. His skin was white, but it turned almost blue at the edges. I think Mafheed had painted it. I liked looking at it—one of the only decorative things in the whole house—but it gave me a dismal feeling. What futile desperation had filled the heart of its artist?

ONE OF THE FIRST THINGS the women of the house did was throw away all my clothes.

"No cowboy," they said.

They had made me a few long-sleeve cotton dresses, muumuu

style except they were black, with elastic in the waist. They breathed well enough, but they were still hot. And they were drab and frumpy, just the way Iraqi women were supposed to look. I didn't really mind losing my clothes. I would be home in a couple weeks, and my dad would just have to buy me new clothes then. I was still in dress up mode. None of this was permanent.

I didn't eat dinner that first night, still struggling to gain an appetite. But I helped the women prepare it nonetheless.

Ahmed's nameless and snooty wife poured some rice out of a canvas bag into a bowl. She set another bowl, empty, beside the first. All of her movements were exaggerated, like I was a child who wouldn't remember any of this. She picked up a handful of rice, and used her fingers as a sieve, sifting the rice, looking for something. I soon found out what: pebbles and little gray bugs. She smashed the bugs nonchalantly between her fingers. Then she pointed at the bowls and at me, and stood there with her arms crossed. I reached for the rice with my right hand and started to pour some into my left hand, the sieve. She grabbed my right wrist and pulled it away before I could do anything. She shooed away my left hand, scrunching up her nose. I went back to work, careful to use only my right hand. Satisfied, she walked away with a *hmph*. I didn't know why my choice of hands mattered, but I decided not to rock the boat.

I sat on a chair nearby while everyone ate in the family room all cross-legged or on their knees around a big oval platter piled high with rice, a bowl or two of some kind of broth, and a stack of flat bread. Everyone ate with their hands. Well, *hand*, actually. The right hand. Curiouser and curiouser.

It struck me that this way of eating around a common platter could have promoted a real intimacy in the right circumstances. Instead, they looked like a pack of hungry animals, still line jostling. The only thing that gave this meal order was the iron hand—the hierarchies of shame and honor. Head of the house first, followed by the eldest males. Women and children last.

Manners were things Muslims put on for guests. But there was no need for those among family, right? Which meant that family members were the ones you treated the worst. They got the least of your energies, the barest of your kindnesses. I thought about my father, giving the best of himself to his clients and his companies. Giving us so little of himself. I couldn't blame him now, looking at his family. He was probably puzzled by our reaction. What he gave of himself to his family was more than would have been his duty here in Iraq. Why wasn't it enough?

I had never felt like such a stranger. I didn't understand the barking language that filled the house. They all acted like I wasn't there. I could rely on the widow for some direction, but she had no affection to give. Grandfather hardly talked to me, maybe because the state of his English embarrassed him, and no family patriarch should have to endure embarrassment in his own house. I went to bed that night believing my mother had been right—I shouldn't have come here.

I woke in the night from loud noises in the dark. I edged up to my door and cracked it open. I was thankful for my door. Mafheed had installed it when this was his room. It had a lock too. I had taken privacy for granted in England. It barely existed here. For a people so obsessed with modesty, they had no concept of privacy. It's hard to keep anything private when so many different family units are packed together under one roof. I could hear most everything in the house from my room. From my doorway, I heard the sounds again, shuffling and impacts, vibrations in the floor. Then a man yelling. Slapping. Tumbling. A baby started crying. This must be Laith and his wife. I was used to these sounds. I had grown up hearing them. In a sort of twisted way, they made me feel more at home. Except that no woman's voice joined in the yelling. Instead, the woman just moaned, her occasional pleas barely audible between the bone and meat sounds, the man yelling, the baby crying, the pounding of blood in my ears. I crawled back in bed and put the pillow over my head.

The next morning, I had to pee. I made my way to the bathroom. I hadn't noticed the day before that there wasn't a toilet. Or a tub. On one side of the room, there was a drain in the tiled floor next to a stool and, on the other side, a shallow recess with a pipe hole in the middle of it. There was no sink. A jug of water, half-full, sat against the wall next to a green bar of soap. I didn't know what to do.

Laith's wife, Rada, came out of their room. She saw me standing in the doorway of the bathroom with my knees together. I guess she understood the situation. She came up beside me and pointed to the recess. I was supposed to squat over it. She looked at me to see if I understood. Her eye was swollen almost shut, a bruise spreading itself out on her face. She noticed me noticing, but didn't seem fazed. I didn't see any toilet paper. I made a sign of wiping my bottom, blushing immediately. She lifted up her left hand, pointing to the water jug, which was looking half-empty now. So *that* was why they didn't handle food with their left hands. As soon as she was done explaining, she turned to go down the stairs to her never-ending duties, hitching her skirt up with one hand to avoid tripping.

As I squatted over the hole in the bathroom, I thought about Rada. She may have been pretty at one time. And fresh. She was worn now, with lines creasing her face, her eyes sunken in when they weren't swollen with bruises, her face gaunt. She never smiled. She was skittish and withdrawing, like a wild doe. Laith beat her almost every day. Everyone knew. You could hear it all throughout the house. But no one said anything about it.

The baby cried all the time. It made Laith so angry, like his weak, shameful, girlish son was doing it just to annoy him. The baby didn't know to stop crying from fear of punishment. Fear just made him cry all the harder. And Laith had no tool but fear to use. No emotion but anger. Strange to see a grown man so frustrated by a little baby.

One night from my room, I heard Laith yelling at his son, trying to get him to be quiet. This of course never worked. The baby was particularly loud and insistent and Laith just kept yelling and yelling. Getting so loud he was going hoarse. Then I heard a *wump* from Laith's room. The wall shuddered and the baby was quiet for the smallest moment, then he let out a piercing cry that turned my stomach. Laith had thrown his son into the wall. I had learned to endure pain for myself, but I had never learned to endure the pain of others. Especially not the pain of the innocent. Hearing that terrified baby thrown about by the one person who was most responsible to protect and comfort him was one of the most excruciating experiences of my life. I didn't know what to do. I ran to my grandfather's room and climbed into his bed. I pulled the sheets over my head and cried myself to sleep. What kind of a place was this?

EVERY DAY, I TRIED TO figure this place out. I was slowly picking up on a few Arabic phrases. I learned the women's chores. I couldn't believe the water situation. My grandfather's house had no running water. There were three blue plastic barrels beside the house that contained all the water the house used for drinking, washing, cooking, and laundry. It was gray-white and cloudy.

When these barrels were empty, they had to be refilled from a well. The electric pump for the well was kept inside, so it couldn't be stolen.

Without running water, chores that would have taken minutes back home took hours. Washing clothes manually was laborious and largely ineffective. The men wore white colored distashas, long shirts that ran down to about the knee. They kind of looked like the pajama gowns men used to wear back in the day. Outside the house, they wore pants as well. Most of the sheets were also white. Off-white. You can't really get things clean without running water. The water in your basin just gets dirtier the more you use it. Everything white took on a dingy brownish color. You washed the whites first because of this. The women's clothes, being black, were always the dirtiest, impregnated with the collected filth of everyone else's laundry.

Cooking without an oven or a microwave took forever too. Between washing things and cooking, the women had little time for anything else. That's why there weren't any chairs in the kitchen. The women had no time to sit down. The washroom and the kitchen were the women's domains, the place where they talked together while they worked. I couldn't understand anything they were saying at first. I couldn't imagine what they had to talk about.

Mafheed talked to me some. He had gone to university and his English was good. He had adopted some English ways. He drank Beefeater gin with squeezed lemon. He did it openly, and no one in the house approved. The family didn't seem to accept him, but he didn't care much. He was a recluse. The family needed him because he owned a store. He provided a little money and procured black market goods. His connection to the family was a loveless marriage of convenience.

I thought it odd that so many families should live in the same house, but I learned that this was the typical Muslim way. Sons were prized because they stayed home even after marriage, bringing their income and the helping hands of their wives into the family. The oldest living male was the head of the household, the patriarch. Women didn't take their husbands' names. They took their fathers' names until they had children. After children, people usually called them "the mother of so-and-so."

The oldest son in the house was the heir apparent to honor and privilege. It made sense that this culture would have dictators and kings. This was just the logical outworking of the family system. Kings and dictators were just the grandfathers of the country—the national patriarchs. Saddam Hussein held this position in Iraq at the time, and the status he enjoyed was singular. Some evenings we would watch the old TV in the family room. The programming was regularly interrupted by commercials for Saddam. He would be riding around in a shiny black Mercedes looking cool in his aviator sunglasses or sitting on his throne in full military regalia, or handling ambassadors in a firm and powerful way. The commercials would have voice-overs recounting Saddam's glory, his accomplishments intoned reverently for the watching crowd. Saddam's picture was everywhere in Iraq, on billboards beside the roads. Painted onto the concrete sides of buildings. He was the regal grandfather to whom everyone owed silent and complete submission.

But everyone seemed to hate him. Like my grandfather in the cab from Jordan, they played the dutiful subjects when they were forced to, but in private their jealousies and their bitterness rose to the surface. I learned later that Basra had been the epicenter of a significant uprising against Saddam after he had been internationally humiliated in the Persian Gulf War.

Saddam had maintained power by indiscriminate public displays of brutal, lethal force. Thousands of Iraqis had died. Basra still hadn't recovered when I arrived there. They learned to fear him again, but they had never loved him. I think about Laith and his son. All these Iraqi sons. And the same dynamic plays out. Sons will fear their fathers until their fathers are weak. They would then crush their fathers' weakness if the strong iron hand didn't coerce them to pay homage. So they take it out on their own sons, and the cycle continues. The violence and shame always slopes downward to the weak; the honor, power, and wealth collect at the top. Iraq had no middle class.

ABOUT A WEEK AFTER I arrived in Basra, my grandfather and Mafheed took me into town. They told me I was going to pay a visit to someone and needed to get a nice outfit to wear. They instructed me, as my grandfather had before, on decorum.

"Walk behind us with your head down," Mafheed said. "Don't make eye contact with anyone. Don't speak."

I had been spending a lot of time with Mafheed over the past few days, and he used the conversations to polish up his English, which before I arrived had grown a little rusty from lack of use. He liked talking to me about places other than Iraq. He seemed to enjoy doing things for me. I feared the other men in the house, and the women all stood behind their men. They had little to do with me on a friendly level. Mafheed was my only connection then to English comfort. English civility. He was portly, his face looking almost water-logged. He had salt and pepper hair and a graying mustache. Sometimes, I could see my dad in him. In his facial expressions. He was depressed when he was drunk, and he drank every day. But we were both outsiders in this alien place, so I was naturally drawn to him for company, though I wouldn't have sought it out under any other circumstances.

The store in Basra was little more than a garage storage unit, a bazaar type place open to the street. It sold rice and flour and vegetables mostly. A few other basic things. Some teenage boys in suit pants loitered about the store. I figured they were the store owner's sons, not yet old enough to help out, idly watching the proceedings until they were old enough to wrestle a few scraps of honor from their dad.

Mafheed had picked out my dress from a catalogue. We were just there to pick it up. It was gold-colored—a stiff polyester blend with a little shine to it—with gold-braided trimming and shoulder pads. It had a very straight profile, the pleated skirt reaching the floor without flaring out. It was a great improvement to my drab black cotton sack, but that wasn't saying much. None of the prices were fixed. After the expected haggling protocol had concluded, we went back to my grandfather's house.

I found out the next morning that I was being taken to see my father's sister, Fareeda. Her name was the feminine version of my dad's name. I wondered if they would be like twins.

As we were approaching my Aunt Fareeda's house, I saw a young girl waiting in front of it. It couldn't be. Layla? My legs quivered as I walked. Please no. No. The girl, apparently a sentry, ran inside when she spotted us. She came back out to lead us in. Such relief. It wasn't Layla. From a distance, they looked identical. I hadn't thought much about my English family since I came to Basra. They already felt very far away. Seeing this Layla look-alike jolted me out of a dream.

"Samaar," she said, pointing to herself.

"Akeela," I said, mimicking her.

She was Layla's age. I felt guilty about feeling relieved that this wasn't Layla. Why should I feel any more defensive about my sister than I did about *this* little innocent girl? Was it better for her to suffer here than Layla? The resemblance had triggered a protective instinct in me. No little girl should have to be in this place. Growing up into what? A household slave? A punching bag? A silent, nameless, automaton? I didn't think about myself. It didn't even cross my mind. My sympathies weren't big enough for my own pain. I would not turn into my mother.

Samaar took us into their kitchen. I was family there too. But Fareeda, unlike the rest of my Iraqi family, didn't drop her manners just because I was family. She approached me quickly, grasped my hand in both of hers warmly. She was a big woman, in presence more than in stature. She did look a lot like my dad. She was loud and full of energy.

"I have waited so long to see you! Oh glorious day! Praise Allah!"

She gestured for me to sit at the kitchen table, which had chairs. This was a woman's house.

"You would like some tea?"

It wasn't really a question. She had already brewed some, and the pale pink china cups were already set on the table in their saucers. I imagined they were not used often. She wanted to make me feel at home. It was a noble gesture. She poured too much of what was probably goat's milk in my tea and dumped a bunch of sugar in as well, giving it one stir before she pushed it over to me expectantly. The excess of milk and sugar was a show of her generosity. Both of these things were expensive in Iraq. I didn't really think about that at the time, milk and sugar being commonplace in England. I just thought about how I didn't like goat's milk, and how it was going to be hard to choke this down. I resolved to drink it anyway. Fareeda seemed like the kindest and most decent person I had met in Iraq so far.

There in front of me was a steaming cup of English tea, a clean little shard of my old life. She sat down across from me, her chin lifting with the cup as I raised it to my lips. I looked down at it and froze, quickly replacing it in the saucer. Floating in the gray-brown contents of my cup, a sugar-fattened roach the color of dried blood struggled for its life, rotating helplessly in the clockwise current. Fareeda looked down at it, and her smile vanished, her cheeks flush with embarrassment and anger. She jumped up from her seat and dumped the tea out in the sink. She filled the cup with tea again, but I couldn't drink it now if I had wanted to. She talked pleasantries with me for a while, glancing occasionally at my untouched cup. Then she took me to meet the rest of the household:

Her husband Sadaaq, the only man in the house. Matsuma, his sister. My cousins, Samaa, Sebeh, Ali, and Samaar. Sadaaq's mother, Beebee, also lived at the house. She sat on the floor against a wall in the main hallway, mostly blind, sweetly soliciting conversation from whomever would spare the time.

I could already tell this was Fareeda's house. Sadaaq said little. He looked like a gnome, with white hair and a round red nose. He walked like a penguin. I found out later that he worked for the secret police, that he had bags of money in his room. I don't know how much of a secret that was. People tell outsiders things sometimes because they think it won't make a difference. After all, who would I tell? But being an outsider more often than not meant things were kept from me, either because insiders didn't want me to know or because, even if they had wanted to explain certain things to me, I couldn't understand.

Sadaaq's sister Matsuma helped me to understand more. She spoke English very well, but she was also willing to teach me Arabic. Mafheed was more interested in practicing his English than he was in teaching me anything. Like Sadaaq, Matsuma was gentle and quiet. Sadaaq's family was a rarity in Iraq.

The kindness in Iraq is odd. It has a passive quality to it, as if the only people who exercise it have been beaten tender by the harshness of their surroundings. As if they are too helpless to hurt people. I learned to distrust grand shows of affection or generosity; they were usually a maneuver. A manipulation. It seemed the only Muslims who showed real kindness, always a subdued and quiet kind, were bruised, broken, and powerless. The aged. The feeble. The disenfranchised. Outcasts. Children. People who had given up on exercising mastery over others or who had never been in a position to try. Seeing a boy grow up into a man there was heart-breaking, like seeing a puppy turned into an attack dog. Iraq afforded me no examples of people who pursued kindness even from a position of power. Ruthless men ruled Iraq. Being on top meant you didn't have to show real kindness to anyone. You were at the front of the line. King of the mud heap. Grace was in the tool bag of the weak, not the powerful. *Abusers, schemers, doormats, and outcasts.* These were the only kinds of people I met in Iraq.

Uncle Mafheed and my grandfather were very pleased with my visit, and things went along as they had at my grandfather's house. The two week mark came and went. I wondered when I would hear from my father. No one seemed concerned about it.

The phone system here was crazy. You couldn't make a call out of the country from your house phone. You had to go into town, stand in line, explain the reason for your call, get permission, wait for a decade while they made the connection… Saddam was very concerned about his people talking to outsiders or leaving the country. The country had to stand behind him. Head down and silent.

Getting calls wasn't much different. The lines were almost always blocked. Mafheed said this was the reason my father hadn't called yet.

"You just need to be patient. Don't you like it here?"

ANOTHER ONE OF MY DAD's brothers came for a visit. *How many brothers did he have?* His name was Akeel, the masculine version of my name, my grandmother's name. Akeel reminded me a bit of someone with autism, slow and gentle, with a simple smile and plodding speech. He had lost a thumb in an accident. When the men were gone, he would spend a lot of time in the kitchen and the washroom making the women laugh. I think he was comforting them in his way. Rada walked a little bit lighter when he was around. He seemed harmless. He spent a lot of time on the roof feeding the birds, especially when the other men were around.

I liked spending time on the roof as well. I loved to see the next door neighbor, Betul, and her daughters. She would see my head poking out above my grandfather's house and she would wave and call out a greeting. I liked hearing her call my name. I don't know why. I just liked the sound of my name in her voice.

Betul's husband had died, and she took care of her four daughters by running a salon. Most of her business came from new brides getting made up for their wedding ceremonies. All the women at my grandfather's house said Betul and her daughters were actually prostitutes. That they made their money by selling their bodies to poor Muslim men who had lost their way. I knew this wasn't true. Betul and her daughters didn't wear traditional Muslim dress. They wore shorts and T-shirts. But they weren't whores. They seemed happy and free even in this environment. They smiled easily and genuinely. I found out later they were

Christians. *Outcasts.* I developed a pretty good relationship with Raghad, one of the daughters. But I had to sneak out to see her. My grandfather didn't want any of his family having anything to do with infidel traitors.

IT HAD BEEN A FEW weeks, and I still hadn't heard from my father. I didn't know what was going on. Then one day, Mafheed yelled up to my room.

"Akeela. You have a phone call."

Finally.

I took the receiver from Mafheed, and put it to my ear.

"Hello."

"Akeela, you stupid girl. I can't believe you'd do this to me. I've told you a million times."

Mother. You know that feeling you get when you reach for a cup of what you think is water and find out after the liquid hits your tongue that it's vinegar? That's what I felt right now. I hadn't prepared for this conversation. I hadn't talked to my mother in a while. Her voice in my ear clashed with my surroundings. I understood a little how my dad had been split into two people. These two realities were unblendable.

"Hi, mom."

"*Hi?* That's all you have to say? You lie to me... scare me half to death... and you say *hi?* What the hell is wrong with you? A skiing trip to Switzerland. I should have known. Well, it sounds like you're alive for now."

"No. I'm actually doing well here. I like it." I was still too proud to let her win this. I wasn't ready to hear *I told you so* from my mother. Mafheed had his head right next to mine, trying to hear my mother's side of the conversation.

"That's what your father said. That you *wanted* to go there. To that hellhole that gave birth to your demon of a father."

"Yeah, well. I like it here."

"You already said that." She paused. "You don't sound like yourself. What's going on?"

"Nothing. I'm fine. Really." I wasn't fine. My mom had picked up on it, but she quickly shrugged it off.

"Suit yourself." I could hear Nana saying it. "Don't say I didn't warn you. You never listen to me anyway. You're gonna get yourself killed. Or worse. And then what? What will I do then? I don't think I can handle more of this. First, my mother. Your dad leaving me for that whore. Now this. No one cares what I think. No one cares what they're doing to me."

"That's not how it is, mom."

Can't you hear me mom? Can't you hear behind my words? Can't you hear your daughter crying out behind this calm veneer, this pride that suppresses the truth.

"No. Of course it isn't. I'm just that crazy woman. I don't know what I'm talking about. Well, fine then. If that's the way you want it."

It's not. I never wanted it this way.

"Just do what you want with your life, then. I don't give a shit what happens to you. I'll never talk to you again."

She hung up. Mafheed took the phone from me.

"Good job," he said. *Good job?* What does that mean? My grandfather was pleased to hear about the conversation. He smiled and nodded slowly when Mafheed told him about it. What did this mean? They were very concerned that I look good for their rich relative, Fareeda. They were happy that my mother now thought I was doing well here. I didn't get why it mattered.

MONTHS PASSED. I STILL HADN'T heard from my dad, and this

trip was feeling less and less temporary with every day. I couldn't take it lightly when I put on my black dress. It was becoming less of a costume. I had come to Basra like a new white sheet, but this life had started to seep into me, a dingy brown. Why was I still here? Had my father abandoned me? I still couldn't eat. Cloudy water, a few handfuls of rice, and some flatbread had become the entirety of my diet. I was losing weight. I was losing my hair. One night about two months into my trip, I had looked down at my brush in horror, a huge clump of hair in it. I was becoming another casualty in Iraq's war on hygiene. Taking baths was miserable. I had to fill a big metal stew pot with water and heat it up on the stove top. I brought it up to the bathroom and sat on the stool over the drain with some harsh soap, lathering a section of my body and rinsing with as little water as would do the job so I wouldn't have to refill my pot. There wasn't a lock on the door, so I would finish as quickly as I could.

Mafheed continued giving me gifts. He didn't know that I gave all the candy and soda in my fridge to Ali and Amaar, the widow's boys. I didn't like the candy bars much. They were some cheap Arabic imitation of good chocolate. Too sweet cocoa-flavored coating over a stale, gummy wafer.

I spent a good bit of time with Mafheed. I started to pick up a few more Arabic words, but I still didn't understand most of what people were saying around me. Or *about* me. My scant knowledge of Arabic meant that talking with him was about the only talking I did. He wouldn't teach me Arabic, acting like it was a lower language or something. I began to think maybe he was afraid that if I learned Arabic, I wouldn't talk to him anymore. No one else in the house ever spent any time with him. He didn't even eat with the family much. His family used him, but they treated him like a leper. I felt like we had at least that in common.

His family used me too. I found out why they were all concerned about making sure everyone outside the house thought I was happy. My dad sent money to my grandfather for me. If my dad found out I wasn't happy, he might stop sending money. Or send me to Fareeda's. Or bring me back home.

Mafheed drank all the time. There are all kinds of drunk people: angry, giddy, crazy. Lorraine was a mixture of crazy and angry. Mafheed was a sad drunk. I felt sorry for him. He wasn't drinking to get a good feeling; he was drinking to keep the bad feeling at bay. To numb himself. I understood the motivation, but I didn't need alcohol to hide my true feelings from myself. I had learned a long time ago how to shut down. How to disappear.

ONE DAY ABOUT FOUR OR five months into my trip, Mafheed presented me with a gift he was particularly excited about: a new nightgown and some lipstick. He wanted me to try them on immediately to show him. I went to the bathroom and slipped on the gown. It was white silk, with a subtle pastel blue floral print in the fabric, studded here and there with gold and silver flowers. It had lace on the sleeves and across the chest. It looked very fine. The lipstick was dark burgundy, a color I would never have picked out. But I didn't want him to feel like I was ungrateful, so I applied it to my lips. The effect was a little over the top, like the makeup I had seen on the young brides leaving Betul's. I blotted some off on a towel.

I came back into the family room, Mafheed's room for the time being. He was slouched in his chair, already holding a glass of gin. When I came in, he sat up a little. I twirled in front of him like a stupid girl and when I turned to face him again, he had set his glass of gin between his thighs so he could clap for me. He said, "Beautiful." But the look on his face was all wrong.

It made me blush.

Just then, the widow walked by in the hallway. She took in the scene and stopped. Her lips were parted and her eyes wide. She started yelling at Mafheed. She looked at me and sternly pointed to the stars as if to say, "Go to your room." Now I was really embarrassed. Poor Mafheed. He had wanted to do something nice for me, and she shut him down. They kept yelling at each other as I climbed the stairs. It didn't feel like long before the widow showed up at my door. She spoke little English. I spoke little Arabic. She was ready to tell me some important things, I could see that on her face. She wiped the lipstick off of my face, as much of it as would come off anyway, and she went behind me to undo the neck buttons on my nightgown. I wheeled around.

"No," I said. She looked puzzled.

"Not right," she said. "Money." She reached her hand high over her head. *Lots of money.* She handled the night gown and repeated that word and that gesture. *The nightgown was very expensive.* "For wife," she said, handling the gown again.

"For whose wife?" She didn't understand.

"Not right," she said, continuing her explanation in Arabic. I knew the night gown was expensive. But it was mine. They had already taken my clothes. I thought she was upset because she didn't think Mafheed should be buying me things that the other women didn't have. I had heard that before. *You can't have it unless Layla gets one too.* But there was something else in her demeanor. She was scared. Perhaps she felt even a little pity for me?

"Ali." She pointed to me, then clasped her hands together. I didn't understand. "Mafheed talk to grandfather. Not right. Not right. My son." She pointed to me again and clasped her hands. I didn't understand what she was saying. She got tired of trying to explain the situation and left.

I lay down on my bed, feeling the smooth cool silk against my skin. I looked at the painting in my room. I had never noticed before, but the man looked a little like Mr. Hutchins, my kind-hearted homeroom teacher. Seemed fitting that he should be drowning. A man like Mr. Hutchins couldn't survive in this place. They would kill him. Or he would become just like them.

There was a knock on the door.

"Who is it?" I said.

"Mafheed."

"Come in."

He entered the room with his glass of gin. He looked a little guilty. Like a scolded dog with its tail between its legs.

"Are you okay?" I asked.

"I'm fine."

"What was that all about?"

"She says it's too expensive."

"That's what I thought."

We talked for a while about nothing in particular. He told me about some book he had read at the university. He sat with his back against the bed. Eventually, I slid down to sit beside him. He finished his drink, and the pain welled up in his eyes almost immediately.

"Mafheed? What's wrong?"

"It isn't fair. They're all upset with me, but what they're going to do... Ali's just a boy. She doesn't even like it. But Hayder says so. And what my father says... But if it's okay for *him*... why not *me*? I told her I would talk to him about it. She says it's final. But she doesn't even like it. But she won't let me be happy. None of them. It's not fair. Who is she to talk to me like this? I told her

I'm going to talk to my father. You should be with me."

"Uncle Mafheed! What are you talking about?"

I felt so much pity for him then. He had become little more than a blubbering child. I hated to see him like this. I had no idea what he was saying. I should be with him? Was he moving away? He looked over at me, with my father's eyes. They were overflowing with unfulfilled ambitions, broken dreams. He leaned over to me and put his lips to mine. I pushed him away, startled. What was going on? His eyes changed, hurt in them. Accusation: *Would I reject him too? Just like the rest of them?*

I didn't want to hurt him. I hated this. He had been nice to me. The only person here that I felt I could trust. He should just leave. We could forget this. *Just leave.* It was tattooed on my face. But he wasn't leaving. He leaned in again. This time, his hand held the small of my back so I couldn't pull away. His lips locked to mine, his mustache pricking my upper lip, the taste of gin in my mouth, his tongue. My stomach turned. I had never kissed anyone before. This wasn't right. I turned my head to break the kiss and pushed him away again, my lips quivering, my arms growing weak. I looked down trying to suppress tears.

"Stop, Uncle Mafheed. Please. Don't do this."

His face changed again from hurt to anger. Was I breaking some commitment to him? Some promise I had made without realizing it? Why did he think this was okay? What was going on? It was the middle of the night. Everyone was asleep, and the house was quiet. Who could I run to anyway? Mafheed was the only person here who cared about me. No one would believe me. *Just leave. Why are you doing this?*

He grabbed my face with his hand and pushed my head down into the tile. The electric jolt of the impact ran around to my forehead. I felt heat creep down from my cheeks, my skin crawling.

My eyes were fixed to the ceiling as his other hand pushed the hem of my nightgown up my thighs, the silk like sandpaper. His hand was hot iron on my skin. A chill poured over my stomach and ran in waves, numbing my body. Then it gave way to a prickling fever. My mind rose and fell in it, my body expanded and contracted in the cycle of fever and chill like a stone suffering a thousand years of changing seasons over the course of a few seconds—crackling, eroding, disappearing. My arms and legs went limp and my breath caught in my lungs. His fingers pressed my cheeks into my teeth. The metallic taste of blood. I couldn't make a sound. Tears ran down into my hair, but I couldn't cry. The lump of it cowered and shivered at the top of my throat. Hot and cold. Fever and chill. I saw my father and mother's faces in flashes, twisted. I put them from my mind. *Just shut it out, Akeela. Shut it all out now.* He pulled himself onto me like a boot pinning a butterfly. His odor stifling. Curry and onions. His hot gin breath condensing on my ear. A sharp thrust inside me, splitting me open. A new numbness bubbling from the fissure. I was splintering like an aspirin in a mortar, the pestle crushing me into the tile. I was gone. Finished. *I give up.* Shattered. Over. And over again. Frightened fragments fleeing each other. Shame and resignation. *Stop trying to piece it together. Give up.*

Then I found myself alone on the cold tile. I didn't know why he left or when he had stopped. My limbs slowly thawed. Spent. I crawled into bed, my arms and legs betraying my weight. The room was pitching and listing. I pulled the sheets out from under my paralyzed legs. I felt mangled, torn in pieces. My wreckage still being tossed by fever and chill. My stomach a stone. My mind sank with it. I looked up. Red and orange light spots danced on the surface above—flotsam. I sank into the cold murkiness. The blackness.

I WOKE UP THE NEXT afternoon. The widow was at my door again. She had knocked on my door two or three times throughout the morning—a distant voice.

"You sick?"

"No. Bad dream." But it wasn't a bad dream. The previous night scratched at the scab of my memory. I had no strength. Stiff all over. The widow came in. I pulled the sheets up to my chin, holding onto their off-whiteness as if they were holding my pieces together. The widow looked down at them. I followed her gaze. Blood. *Oh.* She took hold of the sheets. I shrank from her, the sheets tight in my fists. I didn't want to feel the air against me. I needed to be alone. Looking at her, I felt tiny, insignificant. She wrestled away my sheets, and gave me a look of understanding. *Your secret is safe with me. We women have to stick together. I understand what you're going through.* She thought I was on my period. She had no idea.

The image of Mafheed kept intruding on my mind. Of his face, contorted with anger and then lust. The more disgusting he became to me, the more I loathed myself. *If he had been lovely… If I could make him lovely in my mind… would last night… would I be lovelier then too? Cleaner?* But I couldn't. I thought of him as a walrus-sized maggot, writhing in its own filth. But then that maggot was on me. *In* me. Feeding on me hungrily. Its filth and slime spreading over my skin. I want to die. I had trusted him. This is what my mother had warned me about. About boys. About men. *Dogs,* she had said. He had been breathing over my neck when she had scolded me for my ignorance one last time. But I wouldn't listen. Too proud. I never listened. She was right. My father had sent me here. His brothers—abusers. They used women. Used them up. I hadn't listened. I should have known. *This is my fault.*

My aunt came back with a stew pot of hot water, a scrub brush, and a towel.

"Go. Clean. I clean bed."

My thanks were weak. I felt drained. A cut blister. The blood in me was thick and slow. Time spread out like a pupil in the dark. I went to the bathroom, placed my stool over the drain. Took off my nightgown. This nightgown. How its fineness and smoothness lied to me. I dropped it to the floor. Caked blood, cracked like old paint. On my inner thighs. I sat on the stool, dipped the brush in the bucket, agitated some soap bubbles, ran the brush against my skin. I did it mechanically, forgetting to repeat. I felt the air sucking the water from my skin. Whatever warmth was there was leaving with the vapor. Cold and exposed, I sat crumpled on that stool for hours trying to iron myself out. Minutes passed between each stroke. I felt nothing. My warm water went cold before I realized I had hardly started. I continued anyway. I felt nothing. Nothing could make me feel warm. Nothing could make me feel clean.

When I returned to my room, clammy and raw, I lay down on my bed. The widow had already replaced my sheets, as dirty in their fibers as the last set. I thought about my blood in the wash basin. The sheets going back into it. Never getting clean. My blood would be in those sheets forever. Last night would be in me forever. No matter how I washed my memory, I could not escape it. I would keep dipping down into it. It would recede, but it would never go away. It would be in me, haunting me like a ghost with unfinished business.

My grandfather came in. He had heard I was sick. He said I could have some medicine if I wanted it. He gave me the key to his armoire. I dragged myself out of bed, made the eternal trip to his room. I opened his armoire and grabbed all the medicine I could carry, all the cardboard boxes filled with foil-covered plastic bubble trays. I didn't read labels. I kept myself at a distance. I didn't want to know what I was planning. I shut out the voice in my head that kept asking questions. I watched myself go through the motions. Boiling some water. Brewing some tea in the biggest mug I could find. Pouring in milk. One spoon of sugar. Holding the medicine in a hollow I made by lifting my skirt. Holding the cup in my other hand as I wobbled up the stairs. Sitting up in bed.

I watched myself slide a plastic tray from a box, push a pill through the foil with a thumb on its plastic recess. Put the pill in my mouth. Take a sip. Swallow. Push a pill through. Slip it in my mouth. Sip. Swallow. Push. Pop. Sip. Swallow. Over and over again. I don't know what I was taking. I cleared out trays, dropped them to the ground with all their ruptured foil rimmed craters. Push. Pop. Sip. Swallow. I started gagging on the pills. My throat burning and dry. No liquid could saturate it. My saliva was thick, my teeth filmy. My body numb. Push. Pop. Sip. Swallow. I threw up. I kept heaving. Push. Pop. Sip. Swallow. I felt wrung out. Cored. Blank. Push. Pop. Sip. Swallow.

My grandfather came up to check on me. I watched myself put my head on my pillow. I started to fade. I waited for it to happen. Why wasn't I dead? Then the widow came. Even her boys. Their heads entered my vision as if into a blur-rimmed fish-eye lens, like I was an organ looking up into the face of the surgeon whose scalpel was poised to cut me out. Their words sludged into my ears, viscous and indistinct, pitch-shifted like a slowing phonograph.

Then Mafheed came in, and everything became sharp for a moment. He sat on the edge of my bed. I tried to pull my body away from him. I couldn't move. All my limbs had been disconnected. He moved his hand to my head to caress my hair.

My eyes tracked his movement the whole way, rolling back into my head as he touched me. That hand. His words. Fake words. Like anti-freeze to a wild animal—sweet poison. *Stop touching me. Stop! Shut up!* Silent tears ran down my face again. I tried to shake my head at him. The widow must have seen the revulsion in my eyes. The horror. His tone had been quiet and gentle. Then it hardened when she put her hand on his shoulder to pull him away. He stood up abruptly and pushed past the widow. I think she knew what had happened then. I passed out.

The next day, Mafheed left for Baghdad "to see his kids." I spent the day in the same routine. Push. Pop. Sip. Swallow. That night I went to get more pills. I had to hug the rail to get downstairs. It was like I had forgotten how to walk. My feet felt like they were treading on water, like they would push through the surface of the floor. When I got to my grandfather's room, I couldn't hold myself up any longer. I collapsed on his bed and curled up into a ball beside him. *Why isn't this working? Why am I still alive?* I started vomiting, spewing foamy jets of half-dissolved pills all over the walls and bed. My grandfather awoke with a look of terror on his face, like I was possessed.

"What are you doing? What is going on?"

He helped me to the car and drove me to the hospital in Basra. They rolled me into an examination room while my grandfather stayed in the waiting room pacing. The doctor closed the curtain, which hung from the ceiling in a rounded rectangle. I had no strength. He started to examine me. I watched him cup and squeeze my breasts, run his hands all over me. I was barely conscious. Why were all men like this? He finally called to a nurse, who pushed a tube down my throat, I heard a thrumming and my insides slowly started matching up with the way I felt. Empty. I saw myself on the bed. A husk. My soul had molted.

Gone who knows where. And left *this* behind. All that was left of me. When I went to the bathroom later, I found a little wallet-sized photograph in my underwear. It was the doctor's glamor shot. On the back, he had written his name and number. *Dogs.* My grandfather yelled at me all the way home, my withdrawal egging him on. He called my father, and yelled at him too. I didn't get to talk to him though. I don't know what I could have said then. I wasn't much for conversation.

"I'm too old for this, Fareed. She should just go home."

I didn't care where I was anymore. Where was home? I went to my room. I watched myself break a tea cup, a traditional Iraqi one—like an upside down keyhole. I took a piece of it and started to push it into my wrist, running its edge parallel to my tendons. It wasn't sharp, and I had no strength. I scraped the surface for some time before my thick blood oozed out, trickling down my hand and onto the floor. I passed out on my bed. I woke up the next morning still alive. I couldn't even kill myself.

FAREEDA, WHO HAD NEVER COME to visit, showed up after I got home from the hospital. I think my father may have called her. She brought gifts for everyone: shirts, candy, and the like. She talked with my grandfather in the family room. The next day, she took me home with her.

"You don't belong there. In that house full of men. You come stay with the girls, okay?"

It was a little better at Fareeda's. Sadaaq's family was kind, in the Iraqi way. Matsuma became my closest friend there. She brought me English books and music. Most of what I learned about the culture and language there came from Matsuma. She corrected or confirmed, with detailed patient explanations, what I had been able to pick up on my own, and she told me things

I could not have figured out otherwise. I trusted her. She had nothing to gain from helping me, but she did nonetheless. It was through my conversations with her that I pieced together why I had come to Iraq in the first place, and why my trip had not yet ended.

"Why didn't I just go home, rather than come here?"

"Fareeda wanted you here because it means your father will send her money."

And my grandfather sent me away finally because he got tired of dealing with me. And that's why Fareeda brought gifts. She was buying me. I was an investment. A business venture. Again. I bet she gave him money too.

"But why didn't my dad just tell them I was coming home? Doesn't he send them money anyway?"

"Yes, but not as much. He's been very generous since you came. Besides, you weren't supposed to go home alone."

"What do you mean?"

"You don't know? You were sent here to marry."

That made sense. Was that why Mafheed thought I was his to take, like just another black market good sent from his rich relative in the West?

"But I don't want to marry Mafheed. He's my uncle. It's wrong."

And he raped me. But I couldn't tell her that.

"No. Not Mafheed. Ali. Your cousin."

Ali? He treated me like a sister. I couldn't marry him.

"But I don't want to marry Ali either. He's like my brother."

"And he doesn't want to marry you. I think your grandfather has relented about it."

That was what Mafheed was going to talk to grandfather about.

"So my grandfather knew about all this before I came? My father?"

"Of course. Who do you think set it up? Ali would return to England with you and work for your father."

It was my dad's way of taking care of the widow, his dead brother's wife. It all came together. That guilty look on my father's face at the airport. The fact that he hadn't called me. The widow treating me like her foster daughter, getting up in arms about Mafheed's advances. Amaar teasing Ali whenever I brought them the sodas and candy Mafheed had meant for me. What now, dad? Was this all part of your plan too?

FAREEDA PRAYED EVERY DAY AT the appointed times. Facing Mecca and all that on her custom-made prayer mat. She made a big show of it, kowtowing to the great patriarch in the sky, probably the harshest grandfather of the whole lot.

One day, after morning prayer, Fareeda turned to me.

"You're not the same," she said. "You're not the same as when I first saw you. I thought it was your sickness. But you're better now. What's wrong, child? You can tell Auntie Fareeda."

I didn't even want to talk about it to Matsuma, much less my Aunt Fareeda. Her sweetness was like the coating on the Arabic imitation chocolate bars. Fake. And I had no idea what talking about it would mean. This was a ruthless place ruled by men. What power did some British girl have here?

"I'm okay. I just miss home."

"I was hoping you were starting to think of this as your home."

"Yes, Aunt Fareeda. You've been very good to me. I'm fine."

A week later, Fareeda had an announcement.

"Put on your good clothes. Your Uncle Mafheed is coming for a visit! He just got back from *Bagh-dad*."

She swooned over the word Baghdad like it was the name of some teenage heart-throb. But then she saw my face. She thought she was bringing me good news, some comfort in my loneliness, like when she had made me that first cup of English tea. But this had a cockroach in it too.

She pulled me into the washroom.

"What is wrong, Akeela? Tell me this instant!"

I sat there for a while. I had to tell someone. I couldn't see him again. Not ever. Fareeda cared about me, didn't she? She would protect me if she could, right?

"Mafheed... He... he raped me."

She exploded. The Arabic spilled out of her like foam from a boiling pot. Sadaaq and Matsuma rushed in the kitchen, started calling.

"Fareeda! What's wrong? What happened?"

We came out into the kitchen. Fareeda looked at me and circled her forearm into her stomach like a king's doorman, her upturned hand pointing at her husband. Her cheeks inflated with her rapid breaths, her nose flared, her eyes wild.

As soon as I told Sadaaq and Matsuma, the three of them went crazy, like the angry version of the holy racket celebration, though to be honest, there wasn't much of a difference. Pacing in circles with their heads shaking and bobbing, their arms raised up, they cried out in Arabic. Sadaaq went and collected his gun. He never liked Fareeda's family anyway. Now he had a reason to kill one of them. But he was also afraid. They all were.

"No one can find out," Matsuma said. She explained it to me. Honor killings.

"If a woman isn't a virgin, her family has to kill her to keep honor. The head of the family has to do it. In public. In the streets where everyone can see it."

"But I was raped. Surely they wouldn't…"

"It doesn't matter," Matsuma interrupted. "You're not a virgin. You bring shame on the family name. If they won't do it, they will be outcasts. No one will do business with them. They'll be worse than Christians."

I couldn't imagine my grandfather killing me.

"But my grandfather… he wouldn't do this, would he?"

"If he cannot do it, it falls on the next in line…"

Mafheed. I couldn't believe it. He would do it too. Is that why they were scared? Did they think he was coming for just that purpose? The very man who raped me would then kill me to protect his family's honor, hiding the evidence forever. Just shoot me in the head like a rabid dog while all the neighbors cheered.

The three of them talked for a while in Arabic. I understood very little of what was said.

"You have to get married soon. It's the only way."

"But then everyone will know for sure that I'm not a virgin."

"We have a plan to hide it all."

I was tired of people saying things like that to me. *Tell me the plan! Stop hiding things from me.* But they didn't tell me any more then.

The next day, Fareeda called my grandfather's house and got Mafheed on the phone. At first she was all pleasantness. She didn't want Mafheed to know she knew. She was trying to figure out why Mafheed wanted to come over. Mafheed went along with her pleasant ruse, which meant he probably wasn't coming over to initiate an honor killing.

Which meant he was coming over to make sure I hadn't said anything to anyone, to convince me to remain quiet about it. Maybe he was planning to tell me about honor killings. About how *he* would never do that to me, but his grandfather would. If he ever found out. So I better keep quiet if I wanted to live. That sort of rubbish.

"No, I don't think you will come over," Fareeda said. "No, she's not coming over there either."

. . .

"Who am I to talk to you like this? Who am *I*? Who are *you*? I know what you did, you son of a dog. And if you go anywhere near her, I'll tell dad. What do you think he'll say if he finds out his son raped his granddaughter?"

. . .

"That's *right* you won't be coming over. Sadaaq's going to shoot you if he sees you anywhere near us. And I don't think anyone will miss you much, you pig-blooded sack of camel droppings."

She hung up.

AFTER THAT, FAREEDA TREATED ME like one of her daughters. She bought me make-up and custom-made clothes. Spoiled me, I guess. Felt like me and my dad all over again.

Sadaaq's household was very rich by Iraqi standards. They had running water, which ran along the walls in exposed copper pipes which regularly shimmied, whined, and groaned. Fareeda seemed to like the noise, like it was the sound of money jingling in her pocket. Running water meant that the women had less work to do, hence the chairs in the kitchen. There was a good bit of sitting and gossiping. Lots of idle time compared to my grandfather's house. The family also ate meat at every meal, a real luxury. I still ate almost nothing. I wondered why Fareeda wanted me there for money if she already had more than was necessary. I already knew the answer really. That was just the Iraqi way.

I was learning Arabic with Matsuma. I got along with the girls. Well, all of them but the oldest, Sanaa. She bit the ends off of my lipstick, broke the little beds of blush and eyeshadow into useless pieces, stole my clothes. She was jealous and selfish. Her mother doted on her most of all.

I was shorted out emotionally. Most of the time I was dead, but occasionally, the smallest thing would set me off, shooting sparks. Then dead again. Anything could set me off. Other people's pain. The death of birds. I felt nothing for myself. But if Samaa was unkind to Samaar, it reached me. Not because I could do anything to help. All I could do was know how it feels.

Samaa was like Fareeda. They knew how to get their way. Muslim women don't have the option of violence. Instead, they get their way by cunning and contentiousness, always reading the men they're with to determine the best route. They both knew how to pitch a fit.

I found out Sadaaq's red nose was from drinking. Another male Muslim hypocrite. He drank secretly, but I smelled it on him occasionally. I couldn't blame him. I probably would've used it too by now, but I had lost my window of opportunity. To this day, the smell of it makes me gag. Beefeater gin. Every time I see it, I think of Mafheed.

I had resigned myself to being in Iraq forever. I couldn't leave. No one wanted me to leave. A lady started visiting us then. A simple woman in simple clothes—obviously poor. Fareeda acted like a Sultaness around her, dispensing words like precious favors.

The woman attended to me especially, paying no attention to the other girls. She was giddy around me, and familiar. She brought food when she visited. Matsuma explained that going to someone's house empty-handed was considered bad taste. She also told me who the suddenly regular visitor was: my future mother-in-law. I was to marry her oldest son, Firaz. It had already been arranged.

I had been in Iraq for over a year. My fifteenth birthday had passed at my grandfather's without a celebration. My sixteenth birthday was coming up soon. Now, I was getting married to a twenty-eight year old Iraqi I had never seen. Thanks to Matsuma, my Arabic was getting decent, but people still hid things from me. Sadaaq spoke formal Arabic when he didn't want me to know things. The difference between the rural Arabic I was learning to speak and formal Arabic is similar to the difference between Mexican Spanish and the pure Castilian they speak in Spain.

It was becoming less and less necessary to hide things from me though. Even they could tell I wasn't much of an outsider anymore. I had stopped hoping for anything more than the life I then led. What could I do? Where could I go?

Not eating had taken a toll on my body. My face was fatless, bone-angular, clinging to my skull. I looked like a walking skeleton. My hair had gotten to be in such bad shape that Fareeda took me to have it chopped off. The mass of it looked like a dead animal on the floor. The one thing I had always taken pride in. The one thing about my appearance that I felt made me *me.* Pulled out in clumps. Cut off. Disappeared. What Iraq couldn't tame, it would uproot. And it had been uprooting for so long that the society was as comfortless as the desert it dwelled in.

A TINY EMBER OF HOPE let off a spark when Aunt Fareeda told me my father was on the phone. My mother hadn't heard me. Would my father hear me? Was I even there to be heard anymore?

I greeted him in Arabic, which pleased him greatly. But I could continue small talk for only so long. For someone who hadn't seen or heard from his "favorite" daughter in a year, he had almost nothing to say to me. Nothing of any substance to ask me. It was like no time had passed. He still acted like I was lucky to be here. Like he wished he were here instead of me. *I can't argue with that.* I was angry with him. His nonchalance made me angrier, but I couldn't show it. I wanted to tell him everything that had happened. All that he had put me through. But I couldn't risk losing this opportunity—this chance to get back home. I could hardly stand it. He was the reason I was used up, damaged goods, defiled, disappeared. But I couldn't tell him. But I couldn't say nothing either, or the result would be the same. How could I dislodge his fantasy picture of my circumstances without making him angry?

"Dad, how long am I going to be here?"

And that's when he said it. That I would stay here until I became a good Iraqi woman. And despair broke the last beam of hope over me and my spirit caved in. I hung up the dead receiver, looked in the mirror. It was done. Complete. My life was being planned by everyone else. Ruined by everyone else. I had but one way to exercise control over my life: to try to end it.

I watched myself shuffle into Fareeda's storage closet. Why did my lungs keep drawing breath? Why did my heart still beat? Didn't they know there was no life left in this body? There was a hook hanging from the ceiling. A meat hook. Appropriate. I wrapped my green nylon scarf around it, tied it around my neck, and climbed up onto a chair. I stepped to the edge. I had no words to leave with the world. My life had been crushed before it had started. I stepped off. The scarf cut into my chin. My vision washed out. I felt my pulse pounding in my temples. My lungs and heart were telling me not to do it. They would continue. Why wouldn't I? Why was I giving up?

The scarf gave with a rip and I fell to my feet, buckling over into some bags of rice. Why couldn't I kill myself? I had tried pills, cutting my wrist, and now hanging. I wouldn't die. What was keeping me alive? And for what purpose? I was still that school girl crying for my father. But he wouldn't come. There was no happy ending.

But I decided I wouldn't try to kill myself again. I committed another form of suicide instead. I gave myself over to the currents of my course. I would do as Fareeda and Matsuma told me. I would let my life, what was left of it, float wherever it was directed. And maybe at the end of that course. Just maybe... No. I couldn't afford hope. I couldn't trust it. It was time to grow up.

THE NEXT MORNING, FAREEDA TOLD me that a huge party was planned for that night: my engagement party. She was very excited. I found out from Matsuma that Fareeda wanted her oldest daughter to marry my fiancé's younger brother, but the younger couldn't marry before the older. Marrying me off to the eldest brother freed up the second oldest for Sanaa. And it saved my life. *Two birds with one stone.* Fareeda was a lot like my dad. The poor family I was marrying into was excited because I was their ticket to England. To money. They accepted this less than ideal arranged marriage because they were poor. Their family honor wasn't nearly as important as more rice and flatbread on the family platter. It seemed I was of service to everyone.

There was some kind of religious ceremony at Firaz's house. I was ushered through a room where all the women were, all sitting or kneeling on the floor. I had been given instructions not to look at any of them. Then I came into a room that contained all the men, including the Islamic equivalent of a preacher.

I saw my husband to be, Firaz, for the first time then. He was just under six feet, a bit chunky, with light freckled skin. His scarecrow triangle nose jutted out at the arch, and his black hair had a cantankerous wave in it. He always leaned to one side with his neck pointing out awkwardly at another angle—crooked.

Maybe his parents hadn't mummy-wrapped him tightly enough as an infant. Or maybe his dad threw him into the wall one too many times. Like most everyone else in Iraq, he smelled like curry. His gestures and smiles felt fake and formal. He knew his place. He deferred to everyone, not rich enough or prestigious enough to do any different. He was at the bottom of the grandfatherly pecking order, and I imagine he felt that marrying me might help him buy a rung or two. I didn't like him. Though I took a pretty dim view of men in general at that point. And still. I had given up though. I went along.

There were two cushions on the floor. We kneeled in front of the preacher man in the presence of the other men. I wore the full traditional robe which covered every part of me—my hands and feet and eyes. I was a black ghost. Kneeling on the cushion beside Firaz, I followed the instructions I had been given so many times. I kept my eyes to the floor, nodding whenever a question was directed at me. I could not speak. I could not look anywhere. Whatever. It didn't matter. Fareeda said she had a plan. Seven days later, the marriage celebration would take place.

The night before the celebration, Fareeda told me we were going into town.

"Why?" I asked.

"You must go to your wedding bed a virgin."

I didn't understand. Matsuma explained.

"We are going to see a doctor. He does a little procedure which makes you a virgin again. Don't worry. It will all work out."

I stared at her in disbelief. *This* was the plan? How in the world could I become a virgin again? She told me not to worry, but they all looked very worried. None of this felt very sure. Fareeda spoke up, putting on an air of confidence, like she had witnessed this procedure a thousand times.

"It will be fine. We got money from your dad. We told him it was for wedding stuff."

So he knew about the wedding. He probably planned it. He probably shopped around for the best employee options. I'm sure Firaz took first place in brown-nosing and following orders. We drove into Basra in Sadaaq's car. A Toyota. Of course. I refuse to drive a Toyota to this day. I sat in the back with Matsuma. She held my hand. In the intermittent light of passing street lamps, I could see her face. I took comfort in her hand, but I think she needed reassurance more than I did. Her eyes would dart about as if she expected to see someone she knew. She looked like a spooked animal, trapped in the back of a car, its instinct to escape evidencing itself in agitated twitches. What they were doing was very illegal. I squeezed her hand a little harder. I couldn't stand to see her so worried.

We pulled up to a square white stucco building in what looked like an undeveloped part of downtown Basra. All around this lone cube were empty lots. The sidewalk in front cut off abruptly in the lot next door. The area was dead. Quiet. To good Muslim Iraqis, a place like this feels like a back alley abortion clinic. In the parabolas of light cast by the street lamps, I could see rust-colored dirt scaling the walls.

We walked up the concrete stairs on the backside of the building. I don't know if this office or this doctor had a legitimate medical practice during the day. The waiting room right inside the door was by far the largest area of the building. About twelve metal folding chairs were up against dirty white concrete walls. The doctor's office was also the operating room. It had just enough space for a gurney, a desk, and one chair. It had a small square window of frosted glass streaked with grime. The doctor got out some black thread and a needle, laying them on the desk.

He strapped down my arms and legs with the leather buckles on the gurney. Then he began. Without any anesthetic, he sewed me up inside from front to back. I felt every puncture, pinch, and tug. But I was good at this. I could take the pain, the shame, the exposure. The madness of it. I felt nothing. These parts and particles, accidents and collisions, were devoid of meaning. Devoid of life: just atoms and molecules. I couldn't invest feeling into my life. That was putting coins into a busted pocket.

After the operation, I was held there for about an hour. Then Fareeda and company took me home. They became more and more relieved the closer we got to their house. I became more and more terrified. This part of the plan was succeeding. But what about the next part? If the operation worked, then I would bleed like a virgin on my wedding night. If I bled, I was saved from an honor killing. But what did that mean? That I was sold into slavery to a miserable man that I did not love, doomed to stay in Iraq forever? At least if I didn't bleed, my ordeal would be over. My grandfather or Mafheed would take me out in the street and shoot me in the head. Done. Wouldn't that be better than perpetuating this lifeless breathing? I couldn't decide what I really wanted. Either option held its terrors.

TECHNICALLY, FIRAZ AND I WERE already married as far as the vows and arrangements were concerned. But the seventh day was the "glorious" consummation day. The night before, I had been revirginized. Now, I was to be turned into a fitting Muslim bride. In other words, my body needed to be as hairless as a baby's and my face had to look like something from *The Rocky Horror Picture Show*.

Fareeda had picked out my wedding dress, a tacky thing with huge puffy sleeves—a little girl's idea of dressing up as a princess.

The bridal preparations for a Muslim wedding are like the down payment on the suffering a wife will then have drawn out over the rest of her life. They use threads of string to grab and pull out all of your hair, over the entirety of your body. It isn't like plucking, which pulls out one hair at a time. Threading grabs multiple hairs at once. Every follicle on my body was removed. When they were finished, I felt like every one of my pores had eaten habaneros and tried to soothe the burn with menthol.

The hair on my head, the only hair they allowed me to keep, was shaped into a black helmet. They applied thick black eyeliner around my eyes, drawing the line from the outside corners all the way to my temples. Heavy burgundy lipstick. *Mafheed.*

Firaz's mother showed up during the morning preparations and presented me with a white cloth. I didn't know what it was for. I was to keep it with me until that night.

The wedding celebration was held at a community events center in downtown Basra—a big, barren concrete place. Firaz picked me up at Fareeda's. The car was too small for Fareeda and all of her daughters to fit, so only Fareeda and Sanaa could ride with us. She was so upset about it. Every time I saw her face that whole night, she wore a scowl. She had wanted everything to be perfect. She had wanted all of her daughters to be part of this special once-in-a-lifetime ride. And then Firaz's family had sent this tiny car. Even in this dark hour, I found her childish tantrum rather comical. I needed a little bit of lightness. And whether her histrionics were meant as comedic relief or not, she provided it nonetheless.

We arrived at the center. I had never heard so much noise. Drums, tambourines, pipes, horns, and whatever else people could get their hands on were blowing, blaring, bleating, and beating nonstop. Nothing connected together. And everyone was yelling, their yellow teeth and wild eyes in my face as I pushed through the crowd. It felt like something out of a nightmare. Two chairs were seated in the middle of the big meeting area on a stage. Firaz sat in one, and I sat in the other. His parents stood behind us. I mostly looked down at the floor quietly while the noise swirled around me. Friends and family members approached to congratulate Firaz and his parents. I didn't talk the whole time. No one hardly said anything to me anyway. Sometimes someone would tell me how beautiful I was, but I was not expected to answer. As if the compliment were really intended for Firaz.

Later came a time of dancing for the guests. Eating. Music. They played Madonna's *True Blue* over the loudspeakers, the record Matsuma had given me. It was new to Iraq, but dated already in England, having come out in 1986. The newest things in Iraq were still old by Western standards, like it took a decade for things to get here. But I didn't care.

I sat there, feeling like more of a clown than a bride, next to my husband the stranger, lifted up in front of all these other strangers—all these other abusers and schemers and doormats. And the truth of my life sat in me like poison in a vial. I wanted to pour it out into everyone's drink. But I couldn't. And it sickened inside me.

And right then, Madonna's "Live to Tell" came on. There are times when the lyrics to a song seem so appropriate to your circumstances that you feel like you were meant to hear just those words at just that time. I used to think those things were just coincidences. Eerie sometimes, sure. *But they didn't mean anything.* Did they? Tonight, I wasn't sure. Every lyric seemed written for me. Hearing your own experiences in someone else's voice can be more harrowing than coming to the realization within yourself: like someone you've never met holding your underwear up in public.

I have a tale to tell
Sometimes it gets so hard
To hide it well
I was not ready for the fall
Too blind to see the writing on the wall

A man can tell a thousand lies
I've learned my lesson well
Hope I live to tell
The secret I have learned
'Til then
It will burn inside of me

I heard the song like it was a word from God. Though I never really thought about God. If there was one, he had a lot to answer for. But then these coincidences demanded my attention: the cheapness of my nylon scarf, the dullness of that broken glass fragment, the fact that most of my grandfather's black market pharmaceuticals had been mild cough medicine. Were these meaningless coincidences? Or was I supposed to live? For what? *To tell the secret I have learned.* But what was that secret? That the world was an awful place? That's no secret. I didn't know why I needed to be alive. But something wouldn't let me die. And I knew then that something had to be hidden somewhere deep in the recesses of my labyrinth, a truth that I had buried for its own protection more than for mine. And I would live to find it. To tell it. But not yet.

THE WEDDING CELEBRATION CONCLUDED, AND Firaz and I were now supposed to go to a hotel in Basra to make our marriage official with another act of rape. This one was mandated by law, the other was just protected by it.

We rode alone to the Sheraton in Basra. We didn't talk. The drive took five awkward minutes. When we got to the hotel, wedding revelers had already arrived before us. We waded through them, all still making a holy racket. And then we were somehow in the room. I hadn't thought much about this moment. I had pushed it away, suppressing it. Coping with each new event as it arrived. Now I tasted this night's certainty in my mouth, that sickly taste like the morning you wake up with the first signs of strep throat. I told Firaz I needed to go to the bathroom. I closed myself in and put my hands on the counter. The mirror was a panel of polished steel. My face warped in it. I looked like a zombie clown at some Halloween fright house.

I had no choice. No control. No appeal. The same law that had protected Mafheed now gave me over to this. It was almost worse. Apparently legal. Apparently consensual. I stayed in the bathroom for too long doing nothing, delaying the inevitable. Firaz summoned me every minute or so. Some of the first words he had ever said to me.

"Akeela!"

He already said my name with ownership in his voice. Like I was a pet that refused to be house-broken. Finally, I came out of the bathroom. He was laying on the bed, naked but for his white dress shirt. There's no need for me to go into details. It was a lot like the first time. Just a little shorter. I cried without a sound again, my tears running the track of my eyeliner into my hair, like the makeup had been designed to hide the inevitable tears of a supine new bride.

I bled.

Matsuma had given me rushed instructions moments before

I had left with Firaz for the hotel:

"Put the white cloth under you. Make sure he doesn't see any stitches."

After Firaz finished and rolled over, I looked down and noticed a little black curl of a stitch on the white cloth. I flicked it to the floor. He didn't notice, already drifting off to sleep—a real man. I did not feel like anything but a broken girl. Broken and rebroken like a crooked bone that would never set right.

I took a shower until the water ran cold. It was the first shower I had taken in Iraq. But it couldn't make me feel clean. The dirt owned this place. And now it owned me too. It was inside me. No amount of soap or water could get it out now.

I didn't leave the bathroom. I stayed in there until we had to leave the next day. Firaz hammered on the door for me to come out—my righteously indignant new owner.

Now came yet another ritual in this wedding that seemed it would never end. We drove to Firaz's neighborhood and parked at the end of the street. As we approached his house, there were more drums and horns, like these people had never stopped celebrating. Kids ran out into the street of mud smiling their knowing smiles.

A man stood on the sidewalk at the black iron gate of a spiked fence that ran the length of the sidewalk in front of Firaz's house.

The man held the end of a thin rope that collared a lamb. I had not seen many animals in Iraq. Occasionally, a feral cat or dog would roam the streets, but I think people ate them. I saw very few mammals there. This lamb stood out in this place, docile and quiet amid the chaos. Its brown eyes were so still and deep. You could read any feeling into them: happiness or peace as easily as horror or pain. I turned to the crowd that had started to surround us in front of Firaz's house. Even in their happiness there was violence.

I remembered my father, incapable of anything but anger or lust. He was just a son of this place. A son of wrath. Of sex and violence. Firaz was pulling my arm to move toward the gate. I turned my head. The lamb was looking up at me, closer now. I saw a flash of silver and then blood shot out of the lamb's neck. All the pain I had endured boiled over in my stomach. I barely choked back vomit. I stumbled.

"What is wrong with you?" Firaz scolded.

This place. These people. Firaz held my arm more firmly. We stepped over the lamb's body, still twitching on its side. Its head had turned away from me at an unnatural angle. Its dirty white fur, the same color as my sheets, sopped up the blood pooling on the sidewalk around its neck. Blood just like mine. All part of the ritual.

"It is good luck. For you."

That lamb had died for me? I was the cause of its death. *My fault.* If I had not bled on my white cloth, this innocent creature would not have died today. I would have been the one bleeding on the street. At that moment, I would have preferred it that way. Wasn't it enough that I suffered? Did others have to suffer too? Because of me?

Firaz's parents had bought new furniture—simple wood tables and chairs, all painted black. His parents were very conscious of propriety, painfully aware of how poor they were. Their eldest son had inherited that consciousness. As far as they knew, I was a good match for him. Both families had descended on Firaz's house for the ceremony—the bloody show.

I sat in the middle of the room, an object of honor feeling like an object of shame. I wore a dress made from material the groom's mother had given me, a turquoise silk dress with shoulder pads, of course. It didn't have sleeves. Since I was a married woman now, I was allowed to be more exposed in the presence of his family. I might as well have been naked. Every person there passed the blood-stained cloth around gingerly like it was our first baby.

It was just the perpetuation of a lie. I felt guilty for deceiving this poor family, like I was joining forces with those who had so deceived me—a hurt person hurting people. I hated them all. Did no one have any feeling?

My Aunt Fareeda had her turn with the cloth. She was nearly fainting with joy, a fake smile plastered to her face.

"Praise Allah! Praise Allah!"

I had already begun to hate her. This just sealed it. How could she be so brazen? So callous? Did she not feel any remorse? I was just a pawn in a chess match. A tool for my father. A tool for my grandfather. For Mafheed. For Fareeda. For Firaz and his family. For everyone. I was a helpless agent of other people's happiness, a remorseless happiness that depended on my misery. Unfeeling. Uncaring. And what about me? I didn't feel anything either, did I? Was I becoming just like them? I felt like telling everyone what had happened. But I couldn't.

It had taken me two weeks to talk to my mother when I first started my menstrual cycle. Now I was at the center of a crowd of strangers all handling this cloth and commenting on my blood. On how saturated the cloth was. Like that was some indication of just how much of a virgin I really had been.

After a few hours, lunch was served on a big platter. Lamb. That same lamb. Its flesh took my place in the middle of the room. Everyone jostled for a mouthful of meat: an unusually rich meal for most of them. Fareeda's family had meat every meal, but she still had two lamb chops. She bit into one. I could see the flesh between her teeth as she smacked. Its juices running out of her smiling mouth a little. Animals.

I trusted no one from then on. Matsuma had been there. But she hadn't said anything. What could she have said? Silence, as cruel as it was, was the kindest option. But I couldn't help but feel like she had betrayed me. Like they had all betrayed me. For gain. I was the lamb on the platter, and everyone wanted a taste.

THE NEXT DAY, THINGS SETTLED down a bit. I moved in with Firaz's family. Fareeda would visit sometimes, always making sideways comments about Firaz's poverty. I think she still held a grudge about that tiny wedding car.

"Well, I guess this is the best you can do for furniture. My back is aching from sitting in this chair. . . . Don't you ever eat meat here? . . . Look at that rug. I had one like that outside to wipe shoes on. It was in better shape than that one, but I just got rid of it. If I had known, I could have given it to you. Too bad. . . . No running water? . . . You left my house for this?"

She was mad at me. Like I wanted to get married. Like I had chosen to leave her. Like this wasn't part of *her* plan. And it wasn't me she missed anyway. She missed the money my father would send. Isn't that why she rescued me from my grandfather's in the first place?

Firaz's family wanted Firaz and I to leave. They thought the whole point of marrying me was to give Firaz a chance to move to England. But since my marriage to Ali had fallen through, my dad wasn't too keen on paying for some stranger to come over and work for him. But it was totally acceptable for that same stranger to marry his daughter.

To be fair, I hadn't talked to my father about the marriage. Fareeda probably had, explaining how I had fallen madly in love and couldn't be stopped. In my father's mind, I had abandoned the marriage to Ali because I loved Firaz. What other explanation could there be for my marriage to some random pauper? He was probably thinking, "If she loves him, good. Let her stay there with him then."

Firaz got word to my father that he should call. I don't know how. Perhaps he talked to my grandfather. I don't think anyone else could have convinced my dad to call.

Firaz and his parents sat in the room while I talked to my dad. They spoke very little English, so I didn't feel like they were even listening in. For the first time since my arrival in Iraq, there wasn't any tightrope to walk. What more could be done to me? If my father left me here, things would only be as bad as they had been. I decided to be straightforward, no matter the consequences. My honesty blindsided my father, who had been up to that point drifting happily from one fantasy version of my life to the next.

"I want to come home now, Dad. I'm everything you wanted me to be. I speak Arabic. I can cook this food. I know how to dress."

"Why do you want to come home then?"

"Because I hate it here. I've never liked it. It's a hard life. There's nothing to eat. There's nothing here for me at all."

"Well, there's nothing here for you either. I can promise you that!" He was already getting angry.

"Good. Then if it's all the same to you, I want to come home."

"You are home. Iraq's your home now."

"Dad! I was supposed to be here two weeks! Two weeks! I've been here for *two years!* It's been long enough!"

"You want my help, but you talk to me like this? It's not my fault if you're not happy there. You made your bed. Now lie in it."

"But I didn't make my bed, Dad. *You did.*"

The family could tell things were not going well, and they didn't want to jeopardize their shot at financial security. I felt a pang of regret. Here I was acting like I was the only person in the world. Like what I said didn't matter anymore. It didn't matter for me. I had nothing to lose. But they did. I looked in the old couple's eyes. I was hurting them. *What happened to the quiet girl who bled when she was supposed to? Is this loudmouth, who talks to her father this way, our son's wife now?* I felt bad for them. I was thankful for their sake that Firaz was such an expert toady. He took the phone from me and started talking in Arabic.

"Fareed? Hi. It's Firaz. Your son."

. . .

"No, sir. I don't want to interfere in your family affairs. I just thought I could explain why Akeela was asking to come home. See, I want to come to England with Akeela. She was asking you on my behalf. She's very loyal."

. . .

"Maybe not, but I could help you. I'm a very hard worker. I am your son now. You could teach me. What will you do when you get too old to work? Won't it put your mind at ease to pass on your legacy to your son? I could take care of you. Just teach me."

My dad had always wanted a son. He couldn't resist the logic of it. It was settled. But I couldn't believe it yet.

FIRAZ LEFT A FEW DAYS later, about a month after our "marriage" had begun. He went to Baghdad first, then crossed the border into Jordan. His parents had sold everything to get him there: the new furniture and the rest of their meager belongings. The plan was that Firaz would work for a while in Jordan to get enough money to pay for me to join him there. Then we would leave for

England together. My father could've arranged the whole thing and paid for it too. Or Fareeda or my grandfather. But none of them did.

It was then I realized that my grandfather still had my passport. I could have returned to England at any time if only one male had agreed to escort me. I realized why the West knows of the brutality of Islam only from a distance. Women can't leave without a man's help. As a woman, you can't even go to the store alone. If you travel anywhere, you are covered and silent, standing behind your male escort—some member of your household. Women didn't really leave this place. They contented themselves under the iron fist or they were killed by it. I was often surprised by how adamantly they followed the religion that kept them so servile. Almost none of them were happy—as bleak as their clothes—but what could they do? Before Firaz agreed to take me with him, I was no different. I could have been there forever. No Prince Charming would have come to my rescue. Prince Charming didn't exist in Basra. Or visit there.

Basra was the traditional home of Sinbad the Sailor, one of the characters in the first English version of *One Thousand and One Nights*. Ever read it? The king in the main frame story comes to the conclusion that all women are unfaithful, so he decides to marry a succession of virgins and execute them the night after consummation to ensure they stay faithful to him—disposable brides. Finally, his vizier tells the king that no more virgins are available—the king has deflowered and then slaughtered every virgin in the kingdom. *Sex and violence.* Well, every virgin but *one*—the vizier's daughter, Scheherazade, who volunteers to be the king's last bride.

But she has a plan. She *begins* a story that first night, but doesn't finish it. It's such a good beginning that the king is curious how it ends. So he spares her life. The second night, she finishes her first story and begins another. The king is so enamored with her stories that he continues sparing her life every night so he can hear the conclusions. But the whole time, the threat of death hangs over Scheherazade. One dud of a story and off with her head.

This goes on for one thousand and one nights. Hence, the name. In the span of those nights, the king has three sons with her. At the end of those nights, Scheherazade tells the king she has no more stories. The king has fallen in love with her by this time though, and decides not to kill her. And they live happily ever after. Though it seems such a jealous man would have difficulty trusting such a good spinner of tall tales.

That's how you know you've won your Muslim husband's heart—when he stops threatening to kill you. Every good Muslim girl's fantasy marriage. Yeah. If I wanted out of Iraq, there wasn't much use in waiting for Prince Charming.

AFTER A FEW WEEKS, I left for Baghdad with Firaz's family—his parents, brother, and sister. My grandfather, Fareeda, and Samaa met us there. We piled in a car and started making our way west. I had never felt more anxious. It's like the philosopher said: *Anxiety is the dizziness of freedom.* The whole way, I felt light-headed, almost giddy. What was this? Hope? I thought I had lost the capacity to feel hope. I didn't formulate any plans. I had none. But after almost two years, I was making my way to freedom, whatever that would mean.

The trip out was much easier. Iraqi officers still searched our car, but the interrogations were less involved. My grandfather didn't seem as concerned. They didn't care that some English girl was leaving, so he had a good excuse for crossing the border. Like many totalitarian countries, the Iraqi view was, "Keep Iraqis in.

Keep foreigners out." If I hadn't been with them, it would have been much more difficult for them to leave. But it was kind of a wasted trip in that sense—they were all going back.

My father arrived in Amman before we got there. He had refused to stay in the best housing Firaz could afford with the whole substance of his family's house. My father had called Firaz's place "disgusting." He had moved Firaz into an expensive condo downtown.

When we got there, my father was leaning against the wall outside the condo waiting for the many suitcases of gifts he had brought with him from England for his family. Almost like he was paying my dowry. My marriage and return to England did mean a substantial loss of income for my father's family. These gifts were meant to soften the blow.

I was my mother's excuse to see Nana. I had become my father's excuse to send more money to his family. I guess it would have been shameful for them to receive that much money for no reason. Is that why he didn't want me to leave? It seemed I was the only person who didn't have a plan or use for my life.

Last time I had seen him, I had loved him. Everything I had wanted from him had been real for me that day. But it was a lie. Seeing him now, I had none of my old longings. All of them had been replaced with distrust. For him. For everyone.

But now I needed him again. In order to leave this place for good. I couldn't tell him the truth. Had I become like them? Deceiving people for personal gain. Unfeeling and opportunistic. It didn't matter. I'd have to sort things out later. No time is a good time to figure out who you really are. There are always distractions, reasons to keep plodding along on your present course. But now really was a bad time. The question of who I was would have to wait. At least until I got back to England.

I felt myself immediately falling into familiar habits with my father. It was easier for me to be what I had been than try to figure out some new way to relate to him. I was his princess again as far as he was concerned. But even he could tell things had changed. I had cut off my thinning hair. I had eaten little more than rice and flatbread for two years, and my bones jutted out all over.

My absence had been easy for my father. To keep the money coming in, Fareeda and my grandfather had painted a rosy picture of my life in Iraq. My father wanted to believe it, so he did. He was good at believing what put the least pressure on his conscience. I guess we all are. But my appearance was a flat fact. I saw it on his face—a dim realization of what he had done. Of what I had been through.

"Where's all your hair?" He had loved my hair, handling it often in my youth.

"It's gone."

"Gone where?" he chuckled feebly. "I can see your hip bones, bab." He choked up. I felt good for a moment that he was realizing what he had done. But then I felt guilty for that small satisfaction—that was something my mother would feel, and I was not going to be my mother. Fareeda slithered up beside me and stretched her arm over my shoulders and hung on me like we were old friends. Still playing a part.

"Yeah, always fooling with her hair. And you know how girls are... they just won't eat nothing, you know."

What a fraud.

My father took me to the store with him. I wore my exposed hair in a short pony tail. I could make eye contact with strangers. These small things I had once taken for granted gave me an immediate surge of relief. A sense of freshness.

Jordan had felt so removed from England the first time I visited. Now, after my life in Iraq, Jordan felt like the most beautiful, most free place on earth.

The clerk at the store looked like Amr Diab, even my father said so. I remembered that night listening to Matkhafeesh. *Don't be afraid.* I had a visceral reaction to the goods in the store. How can I describe to you the feeling of seeing a box of Cocoa Puffs? When something so commonplace is removed from your life, sometimes you don't realize there's a hole until it's filled again. I hadn't even realized the holes and ruptures that had formed in me until I reached Jordan. Seeing this box of cereal brought tears to my eyes. My father saw it. It was eating at him. My bitterness toward him started to evaporate. Anger gave way to pity. He had been deformed too. Starved.

He bought me anything I wanted. It felt good to be cared for. It pleased him that this stuff meant so much to me now. Iraq had made me grateful for the only affection my dad knew how to show. So my father went to work removing the poverty Iraq had clothed me in.

"What are those rags you're wearing?" he said, gesturing to the custom-made clothes I had gotten while living at Fareeda's. "I send all this money for you to wear rags?"

"It's not the same as you remember, Dad. These are actually pretty nice clothes."

"Well, they won't do for my daughter."

We stopped at the first clothing store we saw.

"Let's dress up my little lamb," he said. It hurt me to hear it. I remembered how they treated little lambs in Iraq.

He bought me a new wardrobe. My father wasn't shopping for a little girl anymore. I was a woman now. I saw a pair of high heels that I really wanted. The price was extraordinary. My father bought them without comment. I can't lie. It felt so good to put them on. It felt so good to put on pants for the first time in two years.

When we got back to the condo, the family had started to ravage the suitcases. They fell on them like vultures tearing into a herd of carcasses, pecking at each other to protect their claims. Fareeda had taken the lead, the one who needed least taking the most—the Iraqi way. My father sat in an armchair watching the whole thing, his face weary. Did he feel guilty that he was so much better off than his family? Hurt that they paid more attention to the gifts than the giver? Guilty he had left his daughter to be used and abused by these animals? That they had pecked her clean and abandoned her skeleton when she could benefit them no longer? My heart swelled with pity for him, and my anger completely disappeared.

Firaz sat in a corner, bested by Fareeda, lost in this new world, about to make an even wilder jump into England. I remembered what it felt like to be cast into an alien environment. It didn't matter that I thought a day in Britain was worth a lifetime in the Arab world. Firaz knew nothing other than his provincial Muslim life, and I could tell that leaving that life terrified him. He followed me and my father around like a canine phantom, a little puppy ghost that barely existed, imitating us like a shadow and following orders without a hint of demurral.

I jumped into the fray and saved a suitcase for Firaz's family. I couldn't guarantee it would get to them. After all, I had to send it with Fareeda. I sent other things with her too. A backpack, a girly plastic thing, for Firaz's only sister Hibbet, the youngest in the family. Her name meant "gift from God." Her parents had always wanted a girl, and they felt like Allah had finally answered their prayers with her. I couldn't figure out why a mother would want to bring a girl into that place. Misery loves company? I filled the backpack with candy, colored markers, paper, and stickers—whatever I could find that I would have wanted at her age. I sent Betul a tin of cookies with some money in the bottom. Fifty dollars could sustain an Iraqi family for a month.

Before my father left, he wanted to make sure I got a professional haircut and a new engagement ring. The best one Firaz could afford looked like it wouldn't have passed muster as a Cracker Jack prize—a thin, pot-metal band with no stone. Firaz went with us to the jewelry store, saying nothing the whole time.

Though Jordan was not nearly as stifling as Iraq, I was still an object of much gawking. My father noticed people were staring at me, but he couldn't figure out why. Whenever he caught anyone fixing their gaze on me, he would look at me as well, obviously puzzled.

"It's my eyes, Dad. They're green."

"Oh."

Light-colored eyes required an extra covering in the orthodox Muslim world. Jordan certainly was progressive, but the vestiges of their heritage still showed up, planted deeply in the national consciousness. I remembered how my father treated Troy. How invisibly we are all shaped by our homelands. My father took off his sunglasses and handed them to me.

"Wear these then."

That was my father's solution for most problems—cover it up. But what else could he really do? I was offended, but there was no point in it. I could wear the sunglasses, and people wouldn't stare at me as much. Problem solved. But I militated against that idea. Against giving in. I had already given enough, hadn't I? Why should I hide *myself* so *they* could be a bit more comfortable? That wouldn't fix anything. Didn't that just reinforce the problem? My dad squinted in the sun. Whatever I felt about this culture, my father was doing the best he knew how for me now. It hurt him to see how they treated me. It hurt him to imagine how much worse things probably were in Iraq. I put the sunglasses on. *Not for you people!* I screamed with my mind. *For my dad.*

Once we were in the jewelry store, my father picked out a diamond-studded platinum ring set with a huge princess-cut diamond. He took Firaz's ring off my finger.

"What the fuck is this? A fucking piece of tin."

And he broke it in half between his thumb and his forefinger. Firaz said nothing. He didn't even look surprised. He was poor. It was the order of the world that the rich should belittle him. In a way, he took comfort in it—a little taste of home. My dad developed an almost immediate disdain for Firaz, treating him like an unwanted stray that just wouldn't leave. Before we left the store, my father bought me earrings and a necklace, all very expensive.

I began to think there were other reasons for all this generosity. My mother. My siblings. Aunt Angela. They couldn't see me for what I had become. Best cover it up. My father's way. The Iraqi way. But I was sick of the Iraqi way. I wanted to take my father aside and tell him everything. But I knew it would crush him. I knew it would destroy our relationship, and ruin my chances of getting home. But that in itself was the Iraqi way, wasn't it? It wasn't that they didn't know what was going on. It's that they kept it a secret. A dark secret that everyone knew, so no one talked about it. And now I knew, and I wasn't talking about it either. Had I become just like them? But I was forced into it. But weren't they also? I didn't want to think that. I didn't want to give Mafheed a free pass. I didn't want to forgive any of them for what they had done. But they had followed the immovable law of the iron hand. I hated the iron hand, but there wasn't anything I could do about it. It was easier to hate people. But it didn't feel right. Not even then.

Wherever we went, my father shocked the Jordanians with his filthy mouth. They stared at him the way they stared at my green eyes. We would be in a taxi cab, and my father would batter the Arabic language with his English penchant for cursing. The cab driver and Firaz would exchange looks like, "How did this unwashed Englishman learn Arabic?" My dad didn't notice. Or he didn't care. Was this just another outworking of his guilt—this English encroachment on his pious Muslim self? Did he think that in some perverse way he could make atonement for his Muslim sins by defiling his native tongue? No. He had changed. He didn't even realize it. He had gotten a nose job in England, and blood kept oozing from his nostrils. He would wipe it away and curse some more. He couldn't live here anymore. He wouldn't be able to survive in Iraq. Somewhere along the way, he had broken down the wall of separation, and his Iraqi self had become just another colony of the once vast English empire.

The woman who cut my hair stared at it first for some time with an expression of complete hopelessness, her fist under her chin. It was matted together, clumpy, and thin—like a mangy black cat had died with its claws stuck in my scalp. She washed my hair first. Such comfort, leaning my head back into the sink, the cool porcelain lip against my neck. The warm water saturating my hair. Her finger tips and thumbs lathering, massaging, loosening. The shampooing alone was worth the price of the haircut. She sat me in the low chair. She had already settled on a plan, like my hair had told her fingers the only viable option. She cut my hair in an asymmetrical bob, hip and modern. For the first time in two years, I looked like a version of myself again.

I had gone from looking like a wild Arabian orphan to a trendy English woman in no less than two days. And it amazed me how much *looking* better made me *feel* better. I wondered, *Am I really so shallow?* But I didn't care. This was the easy part. I would get to the labyrinth later. I promised myself. But not yet.

MY FATHER LEFT JORDAN FIRST. Before he left, Fareeda and company left for Basra with all their loot, some or most of which they would have to use to bribe Iraqi officials at checkpoints. I didn't feel the slightest pang when they said goodbye. Fareeda acted still like I was an old friend, even a daughter. She cried big tears in her dramatic final farewell. I couldn't believe it. Iraq had taught me not to trust... well... *anything.* Her last words to me were, "Keep in touch."

And I couldn't help but think she wanted the contact for less than social reasons. *It would be a shame for her to lose such a lucrative connection to the West.* But no. I had to stop thinking like this, didn't I? I had to believe that kindness and affection were possible for their own sake, or I would become just like *them.* But trusting people is what got me in this mess in the first place. Why should I trust anyone ever again? So I could be used again? So I could be raped again?

When they left, I felt nothing. It would have been natural for me to hate them all—the abusers, the schemers, and the crushed witnesses to the omnipresent iron hand. But instead I felt nothing. This was the closest I could come to my old self. Hating them would have been a waste of my precious emotional resources, resources that had started trickling into my heart again like black market merchandise. I was almost free, and I would never see any of these people again.

FIRAZ AND I LIVED IN the condo after my father left. I wanted so badly to go with my father, but he refused. It would not be appropriate. Firaz needed me.

"Don't you love him?" my father said.

"Yes, of course."

I had to convince my father I loved him. I had to convince the British embassy. Another link in the chain of deception that had bound me to Iraq, that I might climb now to England.

We stayed in Jordan for another week. Alone. Firaz let me do what I wanted. He needed me now. He couldn't afford to push me away. I started going out into Amman, spending my father's money freely. Meeting people. Finally eating again. I relished the fact that no one knew me. I could create whatever history for myself I wanted. I may have been a broken girl huddled in the darkness, but no one could see that past my designer clothes, my expensive jewelry. I was whoever I wanted to be. I was safe in my labyrinth. A prisoner still. But a safe one.

Once we had worked out all the paperwork with the British embassy, we were ready to go. This made my unofficial religious marriage to Firaz a formal marriage under British law. I had no idea at the time that my marriage *hadn't been* legally binding before, so I went along with it. Anything to get out.

I was nervous when my father left. Was he leaving me here again? I felt reassured when I handled my passport. It had meant nothing in Iraq where I needed a man to go anywhere. In Jordan, I could leave on my own if I needed to. But my dad had made it clear that I shouldn't return to England without Firaz. That I wasn't welcome without Firaz.

Inside the passport, I found the two thousand dollars my father had left for traveling expenses. I hadn't handled any money since I had delivered that roll to my grandfather. Here I was again with another wad of money. This time my own. I hadn't touched money in Iraq. It hit me again what little control I had there. Powerless. And those with power over me had abused it. It was a temptation. I had power over Firaz now. He knew it. Wasn't I taking advantage of that? But this was different. Wasn't it?

I pulled the money out, revealing my passport picture. I hadn't seen it in two years. There was my almost fifteen-year-old self—beautiful, naïve, expectant. I looked at the picture from different angles, then held it up to my face in the mirror. Everything I had been through was summed up there in those two faces. The fresh-faced girl flowering into womanhood—her whole self shimmering on her skin—and the dolled-up skeleton who buried under makeup the bitter fact that her dreams and longings… her identity… had withered under the desert sun like tender herbs.

And the only intervening fact was Iraq.

What will everyone say when they see me? How can I make them understand? I had become an expert at hiding my feelings, hiding myself. But could I find them again? I had learned to block out memories. I had learned to endure pain this way. Now what? I could complain about my lack of freedom in Iraq without having to consider what I would do with it if I got it back. Now I was getting the *freedom* to express myself, but I no longer had the *capacity* to. Because I didn't know who I was.

At night, I slept next to this stranger, hoping he would not reach out for me. I would crawl into bed and turn my back to him. I had no love for Firaz. Pity, but no love.

After the chaos and line jostling of the Amman airport, I was on a plane again. Firaz took the window seat. The plane engines whined and rumbled, and we were airborne, my guts in my throat. We were on our way to England. But my story wasn't over. I was leaving this place, but I was taking it with me. It was in my skin. And I had left the little girl in Iraq. She had been murdered like that lamb in the streets. I didn't know what still lived in this body. My innocence, my youth, my trust, and my optimism were gone. I held the packets of salt and pepper in my hand. They looked just like the ones the Jordanian had thrown at me what seemed like so long ago. But it was not the same hand that held them. I was returning to what I had known, but it was alien to me now. It had remained. I had become the stranger.

Don't get angry.
Don't be upset; it only leads to trouble.

Psalm 37:8

III: An American Mother

WE FLEW OVERNIGHT FROM JORDAN on the red eye. I couldn't
see anything outside the window but the steady crimson
light blinking on the wing. There is a certain tension you feel on
a plane, even when it isn't turning or pitching. You can feel the
snug air pressing in on you. Usually, you don't consider the great
weight or resistance of empty space, but at such great speeds, the
air itself could rip the wings off the plane if the steel gave out.

We landed with a shudder. English morning fog condensed
on the window in the gray English light. It felt so foreign, all that
wealth of water in the air.

We got our bags and went through customs. Most of our
luggage belonged to Firaz. He had brought everything he owned,
worth almost nothing. He had no sentimental trinkets to remind
him of home. The largest part of his wardrobe had been given to
him in Jordan by my father—hand-me-downs that hugged his
round frame tightly.

We came through a set of cream-in-coffee-colored double
doors that looked identical to the ones I had come through those
two long years ago. The chauffeurs, friends, and family members
of all the passengers waited in mannerly layers behind a black
nylon partition. I saw my father in front, hanging over the black
ribbon waving both of his arms to get our attention. Layla was
with him. When I saw her, I knew I was home. That partition
was like the ribbon at the finish line.

Layla looked different. She was a pre-teen now, taller and
thinner. Up to that point, her face in my mind had been frozen

in her youth, unable to update in time with her development. It was like she was a different person. She looked at me like I looked at her, studying me closely up and down.

"See, Layla. Here she is," my father said as we reached them. She had been asking about me constantly, like she hardly believed my father's report that I was finally coming home. The changes that had occurred in her had been linear, normal. The change in me was of a different kind, like my train of development had been derailed and set on another set of tracks. Like I had been steam when she had last seen me, and now I was ice. She couldn't take her eyes off of me.

She tried to hug me. I was pulling my luggage and I didn't take my right hand off the handle. My left hand pressed to her back briefly. She had always been so automatically affectionate. I had never been much of a hugger even before. It had been years now since I had voluntarily offered a physical sign of affection to another person. Unpracticed and still adjusting to the circumstances, I didn't know how to react. She ended the awkward hug, pulling away from me. She looked at my face intently.

"You look so different."

I knew she was right. My father hurried things along, wanting everything to be normal again as soon as possible. He hated beginning things. He hated when things changed. He wanted to pretend this wasn't a new beginning. He wanted to pick things up where they had left off. But I knew that just wasn't possible.

The four of us made our way to his white work van. He and Firaz sat in the front. Layla and I sat on thin blankets in the back. Layla had brought snacks and made a cot. She was camping out. I had forgotten how young she still was: this was fun and exciting for her.

Already weary from the plane ride, I felt like an adult, thinking about how uncomfortable this trip would be—seven hours sitting on my bony bottom on this hard floor.

I looked out the back window for much of the trip. I remembered riding in the back when I was five. I had seen my indifferent father then. Now, looking out the back window, I saw an indifferent England. Layla looked up front mostly. Sometimes she would turn again to study me. I would catch her staring at me. And she would say, almost as a defense, "You look so different."

Once, she told me, "You look like Michael Jackson. And Cher." She hadn't meant it as an insult. But it cut nonetheless. And she just kept looking back at me, the one alien thing in her regular environment. My father's van smelled the same. The English air was still damp and cold. The sky was as I remembered it, still withholding itself. Everything about England was pretty much the same. Yet it all felt completely new to me. And I felt new to it. To them. Well, maybe not new. Just different. *Other.*

My father put on some music. Mariah Carey's "Fantasy." I had liked her once, but the jocular bounce of it and her cheerful vocalizations felt inappropriate now. Layla and my father bobbed and swayed to it, sharing the same moment with different motives. I looked at Firaz with his hands on his knees. Very still. He looked at my father in shock, and his eyes were wide to the new world. Overwhelmed. All the cars, the speed, the highway, the music, the moist air. He was taking it in, but none of this had any place to nest in his mind. He was like I had been coming into Iraq. Now I was more like he was.

My dad was just trying to have fun. To *be* fun. He was playing it all off. Ever since he picked us up at the airport, he had been giddy and nervous. Layla had nothing to cover though.

I envied her ability to get lost in enjoyment. I marveled at the weightlessness of her. She hadn't seen the things I'd seen. My life sat with me like sandbags from a hot air balloon. I would never have Layla's easy grace again.

My dad had bought a house in Fleetwood, right outside of Poulton and walking distance from his new electrical store. We stopped at the store on our way to his house.

David, my dad's right hand man, stood behind the counter. When I walked in, his usually cheery face went slack.

"Keela?" he paused to collect himself, looking me up and down. I smiled, a little sheepish at the intensity of his reaction.

"Why, you're a woman now, aren't you? My..."

My dad cut in, asking him about business, still trying to act like I was the same little girl I had always been. Daren, my dad's other employee, came in from the back. My dad introduced them both to Firaz.

"Firaz'll be working with us now, Daren. Show him around, 'kay?"

My father went upstairs. Daren shuffled off with Firaz. Daren kept looking back at me as he left. *So that's the boss's oldest daughter.* As soon as they all left, David turned his attention to me again.

"So... you're a married woman now. What's that like?"

I shrugged. "You know."

"You seem different."

I was already tired of hearing it.

I had known David for some time before I went to Iraq. My father had bought a hotel from him in Bolton before moving in with Lorraine. David had stayed on to help my father run it, and even after my father sold the hotel, David continued working with him. He was dogged and cheerful, a typical Englishman. He had white hair in a ring around his balding head and a short stocky body. A bit avuncular. He had always been kind to me, a permissive accomplice in my youthful high jinks.

I remembered once, Layla had come to visit me at Lorraine's, and we had spent the day at my father's hotel in Bolton. We spent all the money my father had given us on the slot machines in the rec area upstairs. David caught me taking more money out of the register. I had an impish glare.

"And what are *you* doing?" he said chuckling.

"We ran out of money."

"Gambling again? Tut tut. Your father's going to kill you, you know."

"No, he's *no-ot*," I said in a high tone of voice, smiling back at him.

I used to play pranks on David and some of the guests. He liked having me around. I could tell from his face just how much I had changed.

"You seem… quieter," he said. He tried to correct the heaviness of his tone. "I mean you're all grown up. Last time I saw you, you were just a kid. How old are you now?"

"Seventeen."

"Wow. You're a woman now."

My father came back into the room, still dedicated to keeping conversation with me on a superficial level.

"All right, bab. Time to go. Where's Firaz?"

Firaz came back in with Daren, who continued to look at me curiously.

We made our way back to my father's house. He had a room made up for me and Firaz, but I spent most of the night with Layla.

She kept asking me, "What was it like?"

"It was different," I would reply. I wondered whether it would be better to tell her the truth. But she was too young. How could I weigh down her bright ignorance with the dark truths that burned inside me. But wasn't that my job? I was supposed to protect her. I think about that now whenever I think about Layla. She married a Muslim man later. It breaks my heart to see her in her hijab. I wonder if I could have swayed her from that decision if I had just been honest with her when I had the chance. She won't listen to me now. She thinks I don't understand. That I'm being intolerant, judgmental. If she only knew.

EARLY THE NEXT MORNING, MY father barged into my room talking, as he had so often done in my youth. Firaz was beside me in bed. I was in boxer shorts and a T-shirt—my usual pajamas. My father looked at me, then at Firaz, and stopped mid-sentence with alarm on his face.

"Keela! Cover yourself up!"

I was still his little girl. Was this why he hadn't wanted me to come home? He hadn't asked me to cover up for his sake. He was looking at Firaz.

"Come on, Firaz. Let's go."

My father directed. Firaz obeyed. I hurried to put on some clothes. Did my father not realize I was married? The only unseemly part of this scenario was his unceremonious entrance and continued presence in our room. But I could do little to change his habits of thinking. They were inviolable.

Layla and I spent the day walking the shops on Fleetwood's main street, the same street my father's shop was on. Later, we stopped by. My father took us to lunch, and he introduced us to some of the other shop owners in the area. His demeanor surprised me, a different version of himself for every different introduction. He never told anyone he was Iraqi. He agreed to

whatever anyone assumed. I looked at him with surprise at the newspaper shop. The owner looked at both of us, and asked,
"So, you're Greek?"
"Yeah, yeah, yeah…," my father said. "So how's business?"
The shop owner looked pleased with himself for guessing the right nationality and left it at that. My father was everything from Persian, Italian, Spanish, and Brazilian during our tour of the shops. I asked him later why he did it.
"People look at you differently if they find out you're from Iraq."
So he really had given up on his homeland. He wanted to be only English now. Perhaps that's why Firaz got under his skin—this constant reminder of his past. I understand now why my dad felt that way though. When people find out I have Iraqi blood, they look at me like, "Oh, no! You're one of *them!*" Like I'm wearing a bomb under my shirt or something.
That night, Firaz talked to his parents on the phone. My father sat at the kitchen table of his house, dialing, being put on hold, waiting, getting disconnected. Dialing again, talking to an operator, telling him the extension, being put on hold, waiting, getting disconnected. Redialing, waiting. Finally getting through only to be cut off. He was at the table for hours. Finally, a fragile connection marred by static sustained for just long enough for Firaz to talk to his destitute parents. The whole time while my father tried to get through, Firaz had been raiding the fridge. He kept commenting on all the food. He just couldn't believe his eyes. And he ate and ate and ate. I'd never seen anyone eat so much, like there was a wormhole in his stomach that spirited away all the food before he could feel satisfied.
When Firaz picked up the phone, I expected him to have a heartfelt conversation. But he had nothing to talk about but

food. He went on and on about all the food. My dad had a scowl on his face the whole time.

"What, Dad?" I said.

"They're over there with absolutely nothing, and he's just rubbing it in. What a jerk."

"He's just excited, Dad."

"Yeah? Well, maybe he should hide his excitement a little. It's annoying the shit outta me."

He powered off to his room. My father despised impressed people. The world didn't impress him anymore, and he considered confidence the most attractive air a person could possess. To him, people needed humility only when they couldn't force life to operate on their terms. In his mind, such people were weak. And right now, Firaz was at the top of that list.

Firaz talked for a little while longer, then the line cut out during a dissertation on the joys of sliced meat.

"Baba? ... Baba?" he said, holding the phone away from his ear and looking at it, as if that would fix something. Nothing. He shrugged and hung up the phone. Then he went back to the fridge.

THE NEXT DAY, WE WERE scheduled to visit my mother. Layla had called her. My mother was angry with my dad.

"I can't believe you made me wait a whole day to see my daughter. I've been worrying sick about her. You don't even care. You've been keeping her from me just to spite me."

All the usual stuff. She could've come to the airport if she had wanted. She could have come to Fleetwood too. But the mountain had to come to Muhammad.

We drove to Manchester in my father's white van. He dropped us off in front of my mother's new house. They couldn't be in the same room.

"I'll pick you up in a few hours," my father said flatly. Then he drove off to who knows where. Layla barged into the familiar house and disappeared to her room, leaving Firaz and me in the hallway of this strange place. Layla hadn't thought about it. She probably thought of this place as my home too. But I had never been there before. I felt like a guest, not knowing how to proceed.

I hadn't seen my mother in over two years. The last time we spoke, she had written me off as a lost cause. Then she appeared in the hallway. The change in her was less drastic than the change that had occurred in Layla, but more startling. I had *expected* Layla to change, I just didn't know what that change would look like. But my mother was supposed to stay the same forever. But her eyes had lost their sharpness. Her skin was looser, less supple. She looked tired. She still had that crooked and ironic slant to her mouth, but her lips were getting weary of holding that position. They occasionally slackened into a thin line—a shadow of the future repose some mortician would make permanent on her restless face. Silver had crept into her blonde hair and she had gained a good bit of weight.

My father had warned her already about the change in my appearance:

She's all grown up, Sheree. And she's married. You just have to accept that. She's happy too. So don't go startin' anything. Just let her be. For once in your life. Just let her be.

I would have been touched if I had thought my father did it for me. He was just doing damage control, trying to soften the consequences for himself. Or so I assumed. It was easy for me to assume the worst these days.

My mother looked me up and down. I was wearing an outfit my father had bought me in Jordan: Pants printed with vibrant gem tone squares bordered in black and stacked together like a technicolor mosaic running the length of my legs. I had a tie to match that I tucked into the low-cut "V" of a feminine black vest which hugged a fine, white, long-sleeved, button-up shirt. I looked like a modern woman, especially with my bob haircut.

My mother's eyes narrowed, one of her eyelids less obedient than the other—looking a little like the eye of a stroke victim. I think she was upset that I appeared so put-together. I think she had expected for me to show up at her house a shattered sack of pieces, and she, the faithful tinker of the soul, would then put them back together again as only she could. Except that she *never* did this. It was just a fantasy of hers I think. To be deeply and truly needed.

"Come in. Come in. Well, look at you." She didn't even look at Firaz. She brought us into the kitchen where all the women in my family usually hung out. It reminded me a little of Fareeda's. Women with time on their hands.

Angela was there. *Oh, Angela! I can't even tell you all that's happened now.* I felt my change most significantly with her. We had lost our intimacy. Our relationship had been based on the comforting aunt and the needy divulging child. She had been the tinker of the soul that my mother wanted to feel like. Now I was the mysterious woman with the dark secrets. The old dynamic seemed as irrecoverable as that needy child was—the one who had been cut down in Iraq.

When Angela saw me, she choked back tears. Tears of happiness because she finally got to see me after all this time? Or tears of sympathy because she saw the truth behind the fashionable front? Did she see what my mother couldn't see... that I really was a bunch of broken pieces held together by my appearance? I couldn't tell. But if she couldn't see the truth, no

one else would. Her torrent of questions led me to believe she
didn't see. She asked them without waiting for an answer.

"How was Iraq? How is your dad's family? Is it so very
different over there? You're married now? Is this your husband?
How long have you been married? Is that your wedding ring?
What was your wedding like? Did you like your dress? I'm sure it
was beautiful. You cut your hair?"

She finally stopped. My hair had shocked them almost as
much as everything else combined. My mother sat there with a
smoking cigarette between her fingers. She couldn't sit still.

"Never should've cut your hair, Keela," she muttered.

"Well, I *like* it," Angela responded. Then she turned to me. "I
think it suits you. You never know if you'll like something unless
you try it."

I could tell she didn't really like my hair. But she was being
kind. She thought my haircut was a choice I had made. She
and my mother were still playing out the same rivalry. I felt
overwhelmed. Neither of them realized I hadn't hardly said a
word to them. My mother had no idea how to deal with me. I
think she wanted to appear heartbroken and relieved to see me,
but my appearance and quietness annoyed her. She had mourned
my tragic fate much more effectively in my absence.

"I can't believe you lied to me about Switzerland. You and
your father. Two peas in a pod."

Angela butted in.

"Now, that's not fair, Sheree. She didn't know she would be
gone this long. She couldn't do anything about it. I kept telling
you…" My mother interrupted her, and continued to talk to me.

"Well, you seem happy enough. While I've been wasting away
without a word from your father. Every day I worried my oldest
daughter might be dead. And you have no idea what you did

to Layla. She couldn't eat. It just killed me to see her like that. I almost didn't make it."

"I'm sorry, mom. I really didn't know."

"Of course you didn't. Like it would have made a difference. No one cares about what they're doing to me. Don't worry about it. Just pretend I don't exist. Shouldn't be hard for you now that you're happily married with your own little Iraqi family."

During pauses in conversation, I interpreted for Firaz in a low voice. Every time an Arabic word escaped my lips, my mother would wince. Angela noticed my mother's reaction and continued trying to make me feel better about it.

"You speak Arabic so well, Keela."

"I speak it okay," I said. In reality, I was having trouble thinking in English. I thought in Arabic most of the time. I wondered if I could even tell my story in English. Would my Arabic mind trap the story in my Iraqi experience like a dictator jealous for its citizens? Like a dream, would my Iraqi night become a meaningless and invisible apparition in the English daylight?

I excused myself to the restroom, hoping my father would arrive soon. My mother and Angela immediately started talking about something else. Firaz was there without being there. He was really good at that.

There were pictures in the hallway. Troy and Layla. My mother and her friends. There were no pictures of me. Not even one. *I just couldn't bear to think of you*, I could hear her saying. I saw some new pictures of my mother partying in Greece. Had she taken this vacation in my absence?

My father showed up soon after that. He took us back to Fleetwood. Day after day passed by. I cooked and cleaned at home while Firaz and my father worked. It started to feel a whole lot like

Iraq. One day, I asked my father if I could go get a job. I also asked if I could enroll in college. He said no to college. Yes to a job. I didn't bother even asking Firaz. My father obviously ran things in our household. Firaz never questioned any of his decrees.

AFTER LOOKING IN THE NEWSPAPER, I found a low-paying job as a nurse's assistant at an old folk's home. My father dropped me off and picked me up. I wasn't making much money, but it felt like those few hours out of the house really did me good. The old people liked me. They needed me. I made a real difference in their lives.

One day, my dad called the nursing home to tell me he couldn't pick me up that day. He had to work late. *Awesome!* I thought.

"That's okay, Dad," I said nonchalantly. "I'll be fine."

I rode the bus. Riding in a bus reminded me of that time with Angela. I felt free again now. It was a temporary feeling, I knew, but a real one nonetheless. I took my time getting back home. I stopped by a shop or two, and bought some candy.

On the bus, I met a girl, Allison—a painfully thin, blonde-haired girl. I could tell the moment I saw her that she was a lot of fun. She came up to me and said, "You're so pretty. I just wanted to tell you that."

It shocked me. It was one of the first sincere compliments I had heard in a long time. We talked for a while on the bus. We both missed our stops. She wrote down her number on a torn piece of paper.

"*Please* call me. We should go out some time."

I put the paper in my purse. I was still feeling the buzz of freedom and new friendship when I walked into my dad's house. He had a storm cloud on his face.

"Where have you been?" he snapped.

"I rode the bus. I got hung up a little, and I missed my stop. It's not a big deal, Dad."

"Like hell it's not." He paused for a moment to look me up and down. "What are you wearing? I can see right through that!"

I looked down at my uniform—a classic white nurse's outfit that buttoned up the front and cut off just above the knee. I had white pantyhose, clogs. You know—the works. It didn't seem like my dress was transparent, and I always wore a shirt underneath it just to make sure, but my father's accusation made me uncertain. Had I been walking around Fleetwood in what amounted to my underwear? I blushed.

"You're going to quit your job. You call them right after you change out of those clothes."

"No, Dad. I'll go change my clothes. I was going to change anyway. But I'm not going to quit my job. It's the only thing in my life right now that I don't hate."

My dad was stunned. I had wounded him. Just like my mother used to do. I was sorry for saying it as soon as it had exited my mouth. But I was done. I ran upstairs to my room and packed what little stuff I owned into a little bag. I came back downstairs and faced my dad.

"I'm leaving."

"No. You're not. Sit down." I crossed my arms. "Don't make me say it again. Sit down!" my father yelled, pointing to the sofa.

I straddled my legs off the arm of the sofa, barely obeying my father. He yelled at me for a while. Some stuff about responsibility, how he took care of everything. Blah blah blah. I was sick of hearing it. I had already heard him say it to my mother a thousand times. He acted like I was married to *him* rather than Firaz. So jealous and possessive. I stared at the dead screen of the television waiting for him to wrap it up. He would wait for a moment expecting me to respond, and then recapitulate all of his points in hardly different words. After three or four repetitions, he finally stood there silently.

"Well?" I said. "Are you done?" I had never been this defiant with him. I felt dizzy, intoxicated.

"No. As a matter of fact, I'm not done. I have…"

"Great," I interrupted. "I'll just be going then." I walked toward the door.

"If you leave now, don't bother trying to come back."

"Why? Am I your slave now?"

"Don't talk to me like that! I'm your father!"

"And a hell of a father you've been…"

"I've never done anything but good to you. It's not my fault if you can't realize that."

"*Never anything but good!*" I almost told him everything right then. I had almost forgotten about Firaz. He had been there the whole time. He finally stepped in.

"Everyone just calm down now. There's no need…"

"Shut up!" my father and I said to him in unison. He quietly returned to his recliner to watch the fight.

"I don't care what you do, Dad. I'm leaving. There's nothing you can do to keep me here." I walked to the door, turning toward Firaz.

"You comin' or not?"

Firaz looked at me and at my father. Then he shrugged his shoulders to my father and followed me out.

I called Allison from a call-box.

"Hi, Allison. Yeah, it's me. I wasn't expecting to call so soon, but something's come up. I have a huge favor to ask…"

WE STAYED WITH ALLISON THAT night. Firaz went to the shop the next morning for work. How he managed to stay in the permissive, albeit unenthusiastic, graces of all people amazed me. He truly had a gift for brown-nosing.

Allison lived with her boyfriend, an erratic and irresponsible abuser. They were both party animals, drinkers. They invited me and Firaz to accompany them to clubs and bars. They would get drunk and dance. I would dance—sober, and usually by myself. Firaz never drank or danced. He stood awkwardly in corners and perfected the terminal smile—the smile that was intended to prevent any further interaction.

Allison and her boyfriend would bicker all the way to the club. She would pull me aside, light a cigarette, and talk about what a loser her boyfriend was. He might walk by. She would yell at him boldly, "Yeah. I'm talking about you! Just keep walking." He would curse at her, but keep walking. Later, when both of them were sweaty stupid drunk, he would dance her up into one of those walls papered and repapered over with ads, flyers, and announcements, and he would kiss her roughly and shove his hand up her shirt. Then they would be all over each other in the cab, when they stumbled out of it laughing, when they slammed the door to their bedroom already shedding clothes. We would hear them in their room for a few minutes roughly hacking out the final measures of their animal courtship. Then it would be over. She'd be up in the morning, at the kitchen table with a hangover, smoking a cigarette, and hacking up phlegm. She'd be back to cursing the lazy bum she had slept next to the night before. And he would return it in kind. I could tell their relationship was a fever. And it would soon pass.

After we moved in with Allison, I had to quit my job at the nursing home. I hated doing it. My manager really liked me, and he acted like I had really let him down, like this was the way all the young people were these days.

I started working with Allison at a call center—selling time shares in America. Allison and I spent every minute together. I convinced her to leave her boyfriend. We worked out a plan.

We found a three-level house—a triplex if such a thing exists. Allison got two girls from the call center to move in with her on the second level. I moved into the top level with Firaz. And a lesbian couple, Allison's friends from somewhere, moved into the ground level.

After we moved into the triplex, Allison and I started to drift apart. She went wild. She and her roommates got drunk most every night. Different men entered at night and left in the morning like it was a one-night-stand factory.

I had enrolled in a community college in Fleetwood. I had to take some remedial classes so I could take my high school equivalency exam. Allison, who was a little older than I, was also so much more naïve in so many ways. She had the kind of youthful energy necessary to keep making the same short-term mistakes. I had lost that verve in Iraq. I wouldn't have lasted a week waking up every morning with a hangover. We were in different stages of life, and I began to go out with her less and less. I started to resent her loud music while I was trying to study. I started to talk to her about it, but she didn't want to hear it. She would say things like, "Why are you trying to be my mom? You used to be fun."

So once I finished school, I decided it was time I moved back to Manchester. My real home. I had promised myself that I would do some soul-searching once I got to England. But day had followed day and I had put it off. Manchester was the place though. I would find myself there.

I convinced Firaz to move with me—to quit working for my father. He needed me. He sent all of his money back home. I had to take care of everything for us. And I pitied him.

My mom invited us to stay with her. She had heard about the blowup with my father, and I imagine she wanted to be our savior just to rub my dad's nose in it. Why did I immediately assume vicious motives? I don't know. Maybe because this was usually accurate.

Living with my mom was easier now. I was a woman. She afforded me more space than my father did. She picked on Firaz relentlessly though.

"Why do you always pick food off of Kee's plate?" she said one night when Firaz had forked one of my uneaten chicken breasts. "She's thin enough, you know, without you eating all of her food. And it looks to me like you could do with a little less eating yourself. I'm just saying."

She said things like that all the time. Firaz just stared back at her with silent hatred shining in his beady black eyes. Well, perhaps they weren't *beady*. They were just made a little smaller by the fat folds of his eyelids.

Firaz took all of this pretty well, all things considered. He had never met a feminine force like my mother, and I must admit I liked what my mother was doing to him. She represented the kind of woman of whom Iraq was collectively afraid. It was because of the possibility of women like my mother that Islam had turned Arabic homes into domestic prisons.

One night, Firaz got fed up. I could see the culmination of his frustration building on his face and in his gestures. He was drawing on all the power of his heritage, resolved to make a stand for the whole masculine race. Hadn't he seen Iraqi men put women in their place? He just needed to put his foot down. Or so he thought.

My mother said one last cutting remark and it sent him over the edge. He stood up from his recliner in the living room, gathered all of his manliness into his voice and cried, "I am a man!" But it had come out all wrong. His English still wasn't good, and his thick accent and halting delivery made him sound like a small boy imitating his father. My mother and I burst out laughing, which immediately deflated him.

"Not in my house, you're not!" my mother said, still cackling. He crumpled back down into his chair with a huff. He sulked the rest of the night. I must admit I felt sorry for him.

WE COULDN'T STAY AT MY mother's house forever. I found out from my Aunt Angela what had happened in England while I had been away. Angela had tried to get my mother to do something, anything, to get me home.

"If it had been my daughter, I would have been calling the British embassy every day. I wouldn't have given them any rest. I would tell your mom that, but it was like she didn't want to think about it. She would just mope at her house like you had died. She tried to forget you. She would get so angry with me when I brought it up. Then she went to Greece, and I about lost it. She was off having a good time and you were God knows where suffering God knows what. I couldn't take it. I stopped talking to her. I hadn't talked to her for about a year when she called me up to say that you had come home. I came for *you*, Akeela. But I'm finding it difficult to forgive your mother."

This sat heavy with me. I was glad Angela had told me, but it made it even more difficult for me to live peaceably with my mother. My mother acted like she was on my side. But every time I saw those pictures of her in Greece—her face happy, carefree, half-drunk—I held it against her. *I was getting raped and she was downing her third glass of cheap wine.*

Firaz and I finally got our own place. I worked at a retail store in Manchester, in the Jewish part of town. I made pretty good money. I started to make other friends, and I thought I might find happiness if I could just leave Firaz. I didn't hate him. But I didn't love him either. And I hadn't chosen him. He was a constant reminder that I still wasn't free. My mother told me all the time that I should leave him. But I knew he needed me, and I couldn't abandon him to this alien land. I needed to know he could take care of himself first. So I waited.

Why hadn't everything changed? When I got back to England, everything was supposed to get better. I felt just the same though. Maybe it was England. Or it was me. No. Better leave it at England.

One day, a regular customer came into the retail store. She was a short, wry Jewess with frizzy red hair pulled back into a bun. She was pushing her daughter, a paraplegic, around in a wheelchair. According to a lady I worked with, the daughter had been engaged to a rich, handsome young man—a doctor or something. Her perfect life had been ordered from birth and then she got into a car accident that paralyzed her from the waist down. Her fiancé found some way to make it seem like breaking the engagement was the best option for everyone involved. He had abandoned her. Now her mother took care of her exclusively. It was a sad story.

The mother, Rita, owned a vacation house in Florida. She and her daughter Susan were planning to go there for a couple of weeks, and they were interviewing assistants to accompany them on the trip and take some of the burden off of Rita. I decided to apply for the job. I introduced myself to Rita and she gave me her address, told me to come over to meet Susan. I went the next day.

Susan had shrewd brown eyes, short black hair, and pale, even skin. She was slightly homely looking, but her mind and her mouth were sharp and witty. She hated being waited on. There was a young man also in the running for the job, but Susan liked me more. Rita preferred the young man, but yielded to her daughter. I had always wanted to visit America, and now I had a way.

Firaz, as you can expect, did not approve. My mother encouraged me to go anyway.

"You don't owe a damn thing to Firaz," she said. "Anyway, you'll be back in two weeks, right? What's the harm? He'll get over it. Just go."

She and I both knew that this trip meant more than just a temporary leave of absence. But she wanted me to leave Firaz. No one in my family liked him. He had a job. Now I found myself planning like I wouldn't return even though I kept telling myself that I would. If I had been explicit with myself about my true plans, I may not have followed through with the trip. But I had gotten good at hiding things. Even from myself.

When I told Firaz my final decision, he was furious. He was ironing his pants, his legs bare below his shirt tail. We yelled back and forth for a few minutes. Finally, all the frustration that had been building up in him came to the surface and he hurled the iron at my head. I saw it flying by my head, sputtering steam and hot water as it smashed into the wall. That settled it. I slammed the door on my way out, finally free of any misgivings.

So I WAS ON A plane again. Another two-week vacation to an alien land.

Rita owned a little piece of paradise in Lake Buena Vista. They played the tourists well—Disney World, shopping malls, beaches and pools, restaurants. Susan drove everywhere. They had a completely hand-controlled car.

For the first day or so, things went very smoothly. But Rita's attitude toward me changed dramatically a few days in. I had no idea why. I felt like I had been deceived. Rita started treating me like a servant, ordering me around. She held on to my passport and scheduled every moment of my day. I had gone there under the impression that I would be helping with Susan—that I would be a nurse to her. But Rita started treating me like the help: *clean this, tote that, pick this up*, etc. This was on top of helping Susan wash, change, and the rest. And Rita wasn't kind about it either. Susan kept telling her to back off, but this just made things worse.

It wasn't until recently that I started to realize what had precipitated the change in Rita. I remember now that the first day we were there, we went to the shopping mall. Susan kept giggling.

"What are you giggling about, Susan?"

"Nothing. It's just fun to watch all the guys as we pass by. They're all gawking at Akeela." She laughed again. "Take a picture, guys. It'll last longer."

"Why would they gawk at *her*?" Rita said, not amused.

"Because she's beautiful of course."

After that incident, Rita treated me differently. She was jealous for her daughter, and I think she resented my youth, and my health. Susan didn't resent me though. Rita wanted to make sure after that that I knew my place. It was like she was saying, *You may have youth, beauty, and health, but you're still beneath my daughter*. Perhaps I'm reading into things. But if this doesn't explain it, nothing does. The change was drastic and bizarre. It bewildered me completely at the time.

One day, a particularly weary Rita told me she would take

Susan for a while. She invited me to take a break for a few hours. I needed a break. I had been worn down in the week I had been there. But Rita looked just as worn down.

"Are you sure, Rita?" I said. "I really don't mind looking after her. You look tired."

"No. No. It's fine. Go ahead."

I decided to take a walk. Where was I? Thousands of miles from home again. I wasn't looking at my life from above. I didn't see then what I see now. That my life up to that point had been ordered by accident. I took every opportunity that presented itself as it came. I was still committing that same suicide—following wherever chance took me. But what could I do to stop that? If I had some higher purpose, some deeper meaning, I didn't know what it was. My actions consisted of pleasing the people I cared about. My being consisted of *not* being the people who had hurt me. But did I have my own separate reality, a will of my own? I was just the recess created by the contours of the circumstances pressing in around me. I had an outline—the boundaries where I had pitched my resistance to the forces besieging my life. But I felt empty inside of that. Behind that. I didn't know what would happen if I were left alone. If I had no one to endure, no one to help, no one to love, would I even know how to live? Would I be like that chameleon in a mirrored box—changing colors incessantly just trying to match itself? Had I really disappeared? Had I ever existed on my own terms?

But I didn't think any of this then. I thought about the wind over the dunes, the tall grass swaying in it. Beaches like this didn't exist in England.

When I returned to the house, I passed by two construction workers outside finishing up a remodel. And Rita was furious.

"Where have you been?" she fumed.

"I went for a walk. You said I could take a break."

"Well, I didn't expect you to just go AWOL without telling a soul where you were headed. We got back from the club and you still weren't here!"

"I'm sorry. I thought you'd be a while."

"Why were you gone so long? Hmm?"

"I really didn't think…"

She turned and left the room before I could finish. As she left, she said, "Whatever, I don't need to hear your excuses."

Susan tried to comfort me. "She gets stressed. Don't worry about it. She does this. It'll pass. It always does."

I found it harder and harder to be forgiving. I had already been through enough, hadn't I? And now I felt like it was happening all over again. Here I was imprisoned by this control freak, yet another person who had gained my trust when I had a choice and then broken it when I didn't. Abusers. I think she was afraid to be left alone with Susan. Like being tied down to her without any hope of relief was too much to handle. I was the pressure relief valve on that heavy commitment, and I definitely felt the burden of it.

Rita tried to apologize later, but I wasn't in the mood. I didn't need her. She needed me. I didn't need anyone really. Everyone used me. Rita was just another in a long line. When Rita realized I wasn't interested in accepting her gracious condescension, she started to get riled again. Then I got even more stubborn. I ended a short contentless shouting match by running out through the porch door and slamming it behind me.

The two workers stopped talking when they heard me come outside. One of them had a smoking cigarette hanging from his lips.

"Give me a cigarette," I said to him.

"But you don't smoke," he replied calmly, and correctly.

"You don't know that. Just give me a cigarette."

They were chuckling at my accent. He handed me a cigarette and lit it for me. On the first drag, my head lightened and my stomach floated a bit. *Why do people do this to themselves?* I took another drag.

"She's a little bit of a bitch, huh?" one of the workers said to me in a low sort of voice, quietly pointing to the inside of the house.

"Yeah. I had no idea," I replied.

"I'm Robbie," the smoking guy said.

"I'm Akeela. It's nice to meet you."

"Yeah, you too. You English?"

"Is it that obvious?"

Rita burst out onto the porch yelling at me.

"What are you doing out here? Why are you talking to them? Smoking? You're smoking?"

I was tired of confrontation. I threw my cigarette down. I was about to follow her back into the house and make the best of the situation when Robbie stepped in.

"Hey. Listen. You don't *own* her. What she's doing out here is really none of your damn business. And she can talk to whoever she wants."

Rita squinted her eyes at Robbie, and went back inside. I felt such relief. It was about time someone stood up for me.

Rita didn't let it go though. All night she nagged me about it. And the next day. And every day of the trip after that. It was incessant, like a little dog barking. None of it was terribly threatening. It was just irritating and constantly so.

"Should've picked the other guy. I knew she would be trouble. You can't trust *her type*. Arabs are all the same. This is all Susan's fault. I won't make this mistake again."

I stayed for Susan's sake. And because I really had nowhere else to go.

That last week, I spent more time with Robbie. He was in his early thirties, strong from manual labor, a true country boy. One day, he asked me, "So, do you have anything in England that you really have to get back to?"

"Not really."

"Well, what if you just stayed here for a little while longer. I like seeing you. You could just stay with me. I don't mean anything by it. Just offering. You're free to do what you want."

So I decided to stay. Looking at it now, it seems crazy. I didn't really know Robbie, and it should have been obvious to me that I wasn't even making choices for myself. I wasn't even considering what I really wanted. I lived in the moment, still swept away by circumstances. But I didn't want to go home, so I attached myself to another passing ship in the stream of my life I was so afraid to navigate for myself.

I sent my mother another note:

Dear Mom,
I'm going to stay in the States for a while. Don't worry
about me. I'm fine. Firaz has a job and a place to stay,
and I'm not ready to come back yet.

Love,
Akeela

WHEN I FIRST MOVED IN with Robbie, he treated me like a daughter. I had never learned to drive, and he taught me how. He patiently directed me from the passenger seat as I drove around his property in his jacked-up white truck. Having that rumbling, roaring mechanical beast under my control exhilarated me. I fell in love with driving from the first.

Robbie also taught me how to fish. I remember the first time so vividly. The ripples on the lake shivering in the wind, the rustling of the leaves and the slosh of the water on the shore. The loamy smell of red clay and the deep secret smell of freshwater. Watching the white and neon orange bobber ride up and down on the ridges of the forest's reflection, producing circles of white refraction that spread outward regularly, peacefully, until you found yourself breathing in time with them. Then the twitches on the bobber of some invisible hunger. Then the tugs and jerks. Then the strain and whine of the line that rose and retreated, dripping with the water it had just rested in. And the struggle. Then you pulled the glistening life from the dark and you held it up naked in the light, its mouth gaping, its eyes filled with memories you have no capacity to comprehend.

I still love fishing. Mostly for the stillness and the peace than for the sport of it. Robbie was a good teacher. I grew to love him, but not in a romantic way. I began to look to him as a surrogate father. I assumed he cared about me for my own sake—for my benefit. That he understood what I had suffered and was willing to provide for me, teach me, and protect me. That he wanted to comfort me as a good father should. But he had other things on his mind. Secret things that he revealed slowly over time, not wanting to scare me away. I had already learned to trust and depend on him when I realized that his love for me was more than platonic.

A few weeks into my stay at Robbie's, I got a phone call.

"Akeela? What are you doing? I got your note. Thanks for that. It told me just enough to worry me half to death. You have a husband here, in case you forgot."

"Mom? I thought you didn't like him. How did you get this number?"

"Oh, we tracked you down. And who cares if I don't like him? You made a promise to him, and you're not keeping it. You said this was a two-week trip. You lied to me again. Always your father's daughter." Then she said, "What's that?" as if to someone who was with her. Then, "Okay," and it sounded like the phone changed hands.

"Akeela!" It was Firaz. I thought they hated each other. Now they were best friends or something. I guess Firaz needed another bottom to kiss and my mother needed someone to share her misery. "You need to come home now," he said. "This has gone on long enough."

"No, Firaz, I don't think it has. I'm staying here. This just seals it. I'm definitely not coming home."

"Akeela! You can't do this to me. What will your dad say?"

"I don't care. I'm tired of everybody else telling me what to do. I'm in a good place. I'm not ready to go back to being your personal slave just yet. Or ever again, for that matter. I'm done. I'm sorry. But this was never what I wanted. Goodbye."

I hung up. Had I just stuck up for myself? But at what cost? I got another call some time later. Firaz had told my father. My dad didn't try to convince me to come home. He called for another purpose.

"Akeela, you ungrateful bitch. I taught you better than this."

Did you, Dad?

"You've brought shame on my family," he continued. "You've ruined everything. I'm done trying to help you. No one will ever speak your name to me again. I have only one daughter now. Don't bother ever coming back here. If you do, I hope it's in a box."

Those were some of the last words my father spoke to me to this day. I felt even more alone than ever, but for one spot. But for one person—Robbie. He was all I had in the world.

SOON AFTER THAT, ROBBIE STARTED to make his true feelings toward me more explicit. I felt like I owed him something. The age difference bothered me now more than it had. As a father figure, his age worked in his favor. But as a lover, it felt weird. Wasn't this my Uncle Mafheed all over again? But no. I was choosing this. I had chosen this, hadn't I? So we became lovers. I felt nothing still. My body did what bodies do, but my mind and heart were far away, fishing on a still lake, pulling up secret things that gaped and gasped in the light.

Then I found out I was pregnant. Eighteen years old. Before I had even figured out what I thought about that, Robbie was arrested for violating his probation. I hadn't even known he was on probation. We lost the house we were renting when he went to jail. I had no money of my own. I had nowhere to go again. Robbie's mother said I could stay with her.

She was some kind of black widow. All five of her husbands had died. I don't think foul play was involved, but all five of them were probably happy to go. She's one of those people who can't see virtues in others or faults in herself. A miserable Bible-thumping hypocrite. Her boyfriend, soon to be sixth corpse groom, Craig, was a Baptist lay evangelist. People like him are the reason atheists think all Christians are stupid. I guess he assumed I knew what he was talking about when he said things like, "Let Jesus into your heart." Or "Have you accepted Jesus as your personal Lord and Savior?" But I didn't understand. The only real Christians I had ever seen were Betul and her family. And they weren't like this at all. Really, Betul's family was the only real *religion* I had ever seen. Muslims, Jews, and almost every Christian I had ever known were hypocrites—following a code of superiority and self-righteousness that made them feel a little better about themselves at the expense of everyone else. Craig was no different.

He would come in the room and tell me, "The Spirit is telling me I need to talk to you." He would put his hand on my shoulder like he cared, but his touch was stiff and awkward.

"You're a fornicator," he would say, gesturing to my pregnant belly with his free hand. "Right now, you are under God's condemnation and destined for hell."

"Okay," I would say. Christianese. Blah blah blah. What did this knee-jerk string of tired words even mean anymore? And who was he to call me a fornicator? Just because he hadn't impregnated the black widow, that didn't mean an impartial God viewed them any differently. I heard the muffled and nauseating sounds of their guilty pleasures even over the high volume of the game shows they used to conceal them.

He would continue. "You need to get right with God, Akeela. No matter what you've done. Or what you do. If you believe in Jesus, you can escape the fires of hell. Satan has made a vote against you. God makes a vote for you. Now it's up to you to cast the deciding vote. Are you ready to make that decision for Jesus?"

"Sure." *Anything to get you to leave me alone.*

He gave me some paper with some words printed on it. I began to read it.

"Lord Jesus, I know that I have sinned against you, and that my sins separate me from you…"

I finished reading it. I put the paper down when I finished, waiting for something to happen. Nothing did. Well, nothing I didn't expect.

"Hallelujah!" said Craig. "You're life will never be the same now."

We found out a little while later that Robbie was coming home. "Work of the Lord!" said Craig. "Hallelujah! See, Akeela? This is what happens when you get right with God. Praise the Lord!"

It is hard for me to bury the impulse to despise people like Craig and Robbie's mom. They look down on me. They are painfully conscious of the grace they are showing me if they act charitably even in the smallest measure. Written in their eyes is the assumed reality: *You don't deserve my love, but I give it to you because that's what Jesus wants me to do.* I didn't want that kind of love. I wanted a person to love me because I was desirable. Robbie acted like he would give me that kind of love—that his desire was for me as I was. I thought that would be enough to sustain us even if I didn't love him in that way.

Robbie convinced me that marrying was the right thing to do. He gave me all the good-sounding reasons: *for the baby, because I love you.* The words felt as empty as the Sinner's Prayer I had read. But I believed them anyway. So I decreed my divorce to Firaz—making our true state of affairs the legal state as well—and married Robbie in front of a justice of the peace. No frills.

FOR THE FIRST FEW MONTHS of our marriage, we lived out of Robbie's truck. We drove from place to place looking for construction work for Robbie. He found a fairly regular gig helping to refurbish a hotel in Orlando. While he worked, I drove the truck to parking lots and rested as well as I could. I ate whatever convenience stores sold—chips, crackers, nuts, candy, soda. Sleeping in the truck became increasingly uncomfortable. Every morning, the soreness of my limbs seemed to get worse, like I recharged my batteries every night just a little less than I drained them during the day. I grew harder in my attitude. I was becoming a survivor. Had this happened to Nana too? Living a rootless life. The gypsy life. It made you forget that comfort existed some place. I thought about my grandfather. Nana couldn't enjoy his tea and television. Her spirit had become too restless and indelicate for those little comforts.

We found out the baby was a boy. This relieved me of some of the fears I had harbored concerning raising a girl. I didn't want to be like my mother and grandmother to another daughter in this cycle of mistreatment, but I also believed that bringing a girl into the world was a cruelty. Boys at least had a chance.

Robbie allowed me to pick out the name. I decided on Miles at first, to indicate how far I had come up to that point. But I soured on that name after a few days. It seemed wrong to dump my life onto his like that. I would be doing that enough already. So his name stayed undecided until his birthday.

Pregnancy has a way of making you think about the future and the past at the same time. This person growing inside of me—will he be like me? Will he fail the same way I have failed? Will the world treat him as I have been treated? I oscillated between intense states of hope and despair: *In this child, my mistakes and misfortunes will be redeemed* or *In this child, my mistakes and misfortunes will be repeated.* And the pressure built up inside of me. It was like anxiety and expectation were twins in my womb, elbowing and jostling their living quarters among my organs.

I thought a lot about my mother. Had she felt this while I grew inside of her? Had all of her warnings and suspicions been outworkings of her hope? That was a strange thought. How must she have surrendered to despair when tragedy had solidified as the reality of my life—when her fears were realized, exiling hope. But did she understand that her fears were self-fulfilling? If she hadn't operated toward me in fear, perhaps things would have come up differently. But she knew no better. Nana had done the same thing to her. She had tried to force her daughter to make the right choices, to live a more stable life than she had led. And what came of it? Having invested all of her emotional energy into her fears, her fears alone returned their bitter dividends. And my mother had done the same. Fear. How ugly it was to me in that moment. Someone once told me that fear is the source of all human misery. Perhaps that's right. But hope? I had given up on that. What then?

Thinking about all of this softened my heart toward my mother. Had she not warned me and even guided me in her own way? Had she not been right about so many things? I didn't know how to be a mother. I was young and naïve. I feared I would be the same kind of mother my mother and her mother had been. And I knew this fear would do me no good. I convinced myself things could be different with my mother, and that meant they could be different with me too. I just needed to teach her she didn't need to be afraid. I just needed to try a little harder.

I talked to Robbie about it. I said I wanted him to know where I came from. My mother could help with the baby. I told him I had a dream that the child would be a British citizen. He understood, and he agreed to move to Manchester.

I CALLED MY MOTHER. SHE said we were welcome to stay with her. That I was *always* welcome with her. I couldn't help but think this was just an extension of the Great Argument. My dad had disowned me, so of course my mother welcomed me into her home. But I couldn't think that. Even if it were true, I needed to hope the best of my mother. Better to be duped by hope than duped by fear.

So I found myself again in my mother's hallway with another husband she had never met after another interminable two-week vacation. I was eight months pregnant and tired all of the time.

My mother took an instant dislike to Robbie. She didn't approve of his origin, his country accent (which I had picked up a little by then), and especially his age. She already thought all men were lechers, and even though Robbie wasn't that much older than Firaz had been, my mother talked to him like he was some kind of pervert: *knocking up my daughter and you're practically old enough to be her father.* After two tense days, she told me *I* was welcome to stay with her, but Robbie was not. We had nowhere to go.

My brother Troy had just taken over the rent on the apartment Firaz and I had stayed in before I moved to Florida, and he offered to let me and Robbie stay with him. So we went. I was still the invisible woman whose figure became detectable only by the circumstances that clothed her. Troy has a bruised spirit, but a kind one. One of the first things he said to Robbie was, "You won the lottery when you met my sister. You better be good to her."

Troy also continued to defend my mother: *You know how she is, but she's still your mom, no matter what. This is just the way she copes with things. This is how she was raised. At the end of the day, she's still your mother.* I didn't really want to hear this from him. He hadn't lived with her like I had. She had defended him, protected him. He didn't know what it was like to be completely forsaken.

Robbie found work rather quickly. He was motivated and competent, a get-er-done kind of guy. He became a night guard for a security company owned by a married couple. They made it no secret that they were in an "open" marriage, whatever that means, but I trusted Robbie. I had really no choice but to trust him. He was the father of my child, and I thought he loved me unconditionally.

DELIVERY WENT OFF WITHOUT A hitch. I had almost learned to take my body for granted. My heart and lungs wouldn't quit. I saw more and quicker results with exercise than most people. My body was reliable. Delivering a baby worked out similarly. It was almost like I was watching my body do something impossible. And then he was there in my arms, wet and dark red all over. His eyes shut tight. *Welcome to the world.* When I looked at him, my hope and my fear blended together, and I vowed in my heart that I would never let this child down. I would sacrifice whatever I needed to in order to improve his life.

Angela helped me decide on a name—Max. It's not short for anything. Strong, sturdy, and able to survive in a post-apocalyptic wasteland—just like I hoped Max would be. I chose the middle name Alexander, my Scottish grandfather's middle name. I hoped Max would get the best part of my life and nothing else. I hoped he would be tender and gentle like my grandfather. Maybe some of my grandfather's nature had passed through my mother to me to Max. I hoped so. I hoped my mother still had it in her. I wanted more than ever to love her. It wasn't entirely selfless. I thought *what goes around comes around.* If I hated my mother, maybe Max would hate me. Karma and all that. I needed to try to make things right.

Soon after Max's birth, we got a place of our own. I stayed with Max all the time, our bond growing stronger with every day. I started to get concerned with how much Robbie worked. I felt like he wasn't making time for Max. Or for me. But whenever I brought it up, he got very defensive.

"I'm supporting this family! Did I ask to come here? No. This was your idea. Just be happy I'm bringing home some money, and stop nagging me about it. He's just a baby anyway. He needs you right now more than me. I'll make time for all that stuff later. I promise."

When Max was about three weeks old, I started hemorrhaging badly. I had to go to the hospital, so Max went to stay with Angela for a time.

My mother found out, and she rushed over to Angela's to help. She had acted like I couldn't do anything without her help, and when she found that we were getting along just fine by ourselves, it was like she was angry with me for not needing her. She criticized everything I did: *Max isn't getting enough to eat. Max needs to be bathed more often. You're just a terrible mother.*

I came home from the hospital, but needed to take it easy. My mother stayed with us to help. She sent Angela away. One day, my mother told me about how much Angela had complained to her about having to do everything for Max.

"But she didn't do everything for Max, Mom," I said.

"That's not what she said. She said she's not going to raise this baby for you. That you need to take responsibility for your own life. That's why I sent her away. I told her, 'Look, she needs help right now. It's not forever.' But she acted like you had made your bed, and you needed to lie in it."

"I don't know why she would say that."

"She wouldn't say it if she didn't feel that way. She's just being honest."

My heart sunk. Angela and I had never been as close since I had come back from Iraq, but I had no idea she felt this way. Would she think differently if she knew what I had been through? But she didn't deserve to know now. I thought she knew me better than that. I felt insecure as a new mother, but I didn't want anyone looking down on me. I was doing the best I knew how. So I stopped talking to her. I didn't for a moment think my mother was lying to me. She wouldn't do that, would she? What purpose would that serve?

Robbie continued to be more distant from us. He lost the fatherly demeanor altogether. He began acting like Max and I were a nuisance and a burden. He was at home less and hardly present when he was there. I started to get suspicious. He was going to a whole lot of "company get-togethers" and "office parties." I began to suspect he was cheating on me. And my suspicions were confirmed. He was having an affair with his boss. Her husband apparently didn't care, so she hadn't done much to hide it. I didn't feel much when I found out. I had gotten used to being betrayed. Max and I moved to Troy's immediately. Robbie came over every once in a while trying to smooth things over.

"I've changed, Akeela. I'll be there for you now. I promise. I didn't know what I had with you. I've learned my lesson."

I couldn't believe that. Not one person who had ever pretended to love me had been loyal to the end.

Soon, I was able to move into my own place with Max. Robbie finally gave up on trying to reconcile our relationship and went back to the States.

I had nothing, no one, but Max. We were dependent on each other. I felt like I was as much a baby as he was. My next door neighbor Donna, who was also a single mother, taught me some of the things she had picked up over the years about taking care of children. My mother had criticized me, but she had never been willing to teach me how to do anything. If she saw me making Max's formula or changing his diaper, she would just step in with a curt, "You're not doing that right." Then she would do it herself without explanation, cooing at Max the whole time like I didn't exist. Like I didn't *need* to exist. It felt like being in Iraq. Again. But Donna explained things to me. She helped me become a more confident mother.

THEN I MET SIMON—HALF-IRISH, HALF-ITALIAN, handsome and smart. I met him in a park near my flat. He immediately warmed to Max. We talked for a while. He worked as a fund raiser for a charity. *Of course.* He was so chivalrous and kind. He seemed like the perfect guy. But he had a girlfriend. If he had any romantic feelings toward me, he didn't show them.

We started to hang out occasionally. Then I met his girlfriend. He confided in me. I didn't know why he liked spending time with me. I was just a used-up single mother—damaged goods. I felt below him on every level.

One day, I saw his girlfriend having a picnic in the park with another man. It looked a little more than friendly from the way they were touching each other. I called Simon. He had suspected she was secretly dating her lab partner. When he confronted her, she confessed to everything and left him. Strange. I could have clung to a guy like Simon to the end, come what may. Women never seem to understand what they have in a good man. Nana hadn't appreciated my grandfather. This woman had run around on Simon. No wonder good men were hard to find. Being good had to be its own reward, because it looked like good people couldn't expect any other reward.

I thought maybe Simon might ask me out now. But he didn't. He told me a few weeks later that he had accepted a job in the south of France, living on a farm and working on hot-air balloons or something. It seemed a fitting occupation for him. Picturesque. I wanted to ask if we could come with him, but

I didn't. Even now, I don't have any idea how he would have responded if I had asked. Did he withhold romance because he thought it was too much to ask of me: he didn't want to steal away some of my heart from Max? Or did he think of me as I thought of myself—as unworthy. I assumed the latter. He left. My heart broke. But experience chided me: *Well, what did you expect, Akeela? Did you think a guy like that would want to be with a woman like you? Get real.*

Max was a little over fourteen months when Robbie called again.

"Keela. Hey. How's it going?"

"It's going."

"Good. Good. You're probably wondering why I'm calling you, so I'll just cut to the chase. I've been thinking a lot about you. And I want to see you. And I want to see my son."

We talked for a while. What did I have left here? Robbie *was* Max's father. Robbie and I were better matched for one another. We were both broken people. I belonged with a guy like Robbie. I couldn't expect any more. Simon had confirmed this. So I agreed to move back in with him. To come back to America.

His new house was a step up from my flat in England. He was working construction again, but he took that first day off to be with us. He was more like the Robbie from before. He played with Max, lifting him into the air. After a few minutes, Robbie had run out of fatherly things to do with Max, so he focused his attention on me.

"It's good to have you back," he said. "You look good."

I did look better. My time in Iraq felt remote, like it had happened to another person—to a girl I had once known.

Three days after I arrived, someone was banging on the door.

Robbie had gone back to work. I ran to the door, hoping the noise wouldn't wake Max up from his nap.

At the door was a dirty-looking drunk with a kid on her hip and another one hanging on her sweatshirt. She reminded me of Lorraine—she smelled like yeast and malt liquor.

"Who're *you?*" she said in a thick, slurred redneck voice.

"Who are you?" I replied.

"Robbie's girlfriend." *What?*

"Really? Well, I'm Robbie's *wife.*"

"Well ain't you just a dandy ol' gal. Where's Robbie?"

"At work. What do you want?"

"He kicked me out, but I ain't got no place to go. We was fixin' to get married. I love 'im. I jus' love 'im. An' I don't know what I'd do 'thout 'im. I know I'd be good to 'im. I was there. When you cast 'im off. *I* was the one who took care of 'im then. And when you leave again, I'm uh be there."

She started to tear up. Drunk tears. I had seen them before, but I still felt sorry for her.

"Do you want to come in?" I said.

"Sure." She sat on the couch. I got her a glass of ice water.

"Thanks. I hate this for you. You seem nice."

What did I know? She was trashy, but she seemed to care more about Robbie than I did. Especially right then. I despised him at that moment. He had used her up and kicked her out just in time to replace her with a fresh body—another woman stupid enough to trust him. Again. Now he would use me up and toss me away too? Uh-uh. Not again. They deserved each other.

"No, no, that's fine." I said. "For all I care, you can *have* him. But look, I need a day or two to work things out. Just to find somewhere else to stay and all that. Can you give me just a couple of days?"

"Sure. You're so sweet. You don't know what this means to me." She fawned over me crying. It took a good bit of work to get her out of the door.

When she left with her kids, everything I had been blocking came to the surface. *Why? Why was everything in my life such utter total misery? Just when I had anything at all, it was snatched from my hands. Was it me?*

I went into a rage, kicking over chairs, throwing lamps into the wall, smashing cups and plates... I destroyed everything I could get my hands on. Then I heard Max wailing from his room. I calmed down. That's right. Not everything was misery. I still had Max. But what to do? I obviously couldn't stay there. I smiled when I imagined Robbie coming home to this mess to find us gone.

I pawned my wedding rings, all my jewelry, even the Jordanian treasures my father had used to dress up "his little lamb." I would just go back to England. I'd figure *something* out. But there was no reason to stay *here*. Problem was, I had left our passports at Robbie's. I called Robbie to set up a meeting. Robbie told me he just wanted to see his son one more time, then we could leave.

When I showed up a couple days later, the drunken ragamuffin answered the door. *Well, well.* He had probably called her as soon as he came home. She probably cleared up my mess. It hadn't cost him anything.

"What do *you* want?" she said, with the haughty air of a mistress who has displaced a wife. Her set jaw and pursed lips said, *I may not be prettier than you. Or as fine and proper. But I've still got your man.* Lorraine and Sheree all over again. Except I didn't care to play that game. I just wanted our passports so I could leave. Robbie came and stood in the doorway.

"All right, I'll get your stuff," he said. "But first I want to hold my son for a little while."

"Fine," I said, gently transferring Max to his father's arms.

"Aww. Don't you look just like your Daddy, little man? Yes you do. Yes you do. And it's a good thing too."

It didn't take long for it to seem like this visit needed to end. Robbie kept trying to use Max to hurt me.

"All right, Robbie. Cut it out. Let's have him back, and go get our passports."

"Mommy didn't say please. Mean mommy." He waved Max's hand at me as he said it again: "Mean mommy."

"Stop, Robbie. Just give him to me."

He glared at me. His eyes were so twisted. They had hurt and malice in them.

"Give him to me, Robbie. *Please.*"

"Naw," he said simply, clicking his molars together on the word. "I think I'll just hold onto him for a while." He went inside with Max, backing in with this queer smirk on his face. He closed the door, and I heard the bolt slide into place. I stood there dumb-founded. *What had just happened?* Then I started banging on the door.

"Robbie!" I yelled. "Robbie. This isn't funny. Robbie! Give me my son back! Robbie, you sunnuhvabitch."

I yelled for a while. The neighbors called the cops. Or Robbie did. I don't know. But the police came. I ran up to them basically hysterical. Each of them held one arm out and put their other arms on their guns.

"Stop. You need to calm down, ma'am. What's the problem?"

"He took my son. He has my son."

"Who has your son?"

"My husband. We're separated. He took my son. He won't give him back."

"Is your husband the father of the child?"

"Who cares? It doesn't matter. He's got my son and I'm not leaving without him. That bastard has my son. Are you hearing what I'm saying?"

"We're just trying to establish what's going on here, ma'am. You need to calm down. We're here to help. We'll just get your husband out here to have a little talk." They knocked on the door. "Hello? Orange County police. We'd like to talk to you."

Robbie came to the door holding Max, looking very surprised.

"What's this about, officers?" he said calmly.

"This woman says you took her son."

"*Our* son, yes. I have him for his own safety. His mother isn't stable right now. She leaves him alone here for hours. She just wrecked the place completely. I came in here and everything was smashed up. She had gotten some kind of drunk again and she just left him here. I'm not willing to let her have him back. Not again. It just isn't safe. She's just been acting so crazy, you know. It's just not a good environment for the little guy."

The police turned to me.

"That's not true," I said. "I just got here. Max was never alone. He was with me. He's lying."

The police looked inside. The ragamuffin hadn't cleaned up at all. They had planned to do this.

"His place does look to be in pretty bad shape. Is it true that you are responsible for that, ma'am?"

"Yes, officers." My voice started to rise. "But I wasn't drunk, I was just…"

"That's enough. Don't get all excited. We hear you." The main officer paused for a little while. He spoke into the communicator on his shoulder. Then he turned to me.

"Look. I'm sorry, but this is the boy's father. You both have a right to custody right now, and I don't see any compelling reason why I should give the boy to you. You admitted to doing damage to this man's property, and frankly, you don't seem emotionally stable. The father has possession of the child right now, so…"

"You can't do this!" I cried.

"Excuse me?" the officer retorted.

"We're not even American citizens. We're both British. I can prove it. Robbie has our passports and Max's birth certificate in there proving it."

"If you want your passport, I'll be happy to get it," Robbie said. Was he inviting me to leave the country?

"I'm not leaving without Max," I said.

"You don't have a choice, ma'am," the police officer said. "You can leave here of your own free will or you can leave in cuffs. It's your choice. Go file for custody and let a judge figure this out, but this is over for now."

"I can't. I won't." The strength emptied out of my voice.

"Like I said. You can leave the easy way or the hard way. Which will it be?" the officer replied.

Robbie came back with my passport.

"Here you go. No hard feelings." He said it for the sake of the police. I looked like a crazy she-bear. He looked like the calm competent father who had made an unfortunate choice of marriage partners. There was nothing I could do. In Iraq, the law had protected abusers and further victimized the helpless. I had expected the land of the free to be different. But it wasn't.

I STILL HAD SOME MONEY left from pawning my jewelry, so I stayed in hotels and wherever I was welcome. I was running out of money quickly. I looked up some lawyers in the phone book to ask about regaining custody of Max. All of them required an up-front retainer that I didn't have, and their hourly rates were ludicrous. I didn't have enough money to pay for justice.

I also couldn't find any work. I was a British citizen with no green card, no work permit, no permanent residence, no driver's license, no car... no nothing. I didn't even have Max now.

Robbie put Max in day care—a drab mercenary place employing a bunch of fake smilers. They wouldn't let me see him. Robbie had made it out like I was a violent criminal or something. When I stormed in demanding to see Max, they threatened to call the police if I didn't leave immediately. They escorted me out of the building, and on my way, I saw Max for just a moment through a glass observation window. My son. The only thing in the world I had to live for. I had to get him back. That image of him in this place filled me with absolute resolve. I would do whatever I had to, but I would earn money and get him back. No matter what it took.

But what could I do? I needed money. I needed it now. Reputable work was not available to me. Reader, don't judge me for what I did next. What would you have done in my shoes?

There was a strip club in town. I had driven by it in disgust so many times. Now I felt like it might be my only option. Nervous and sick to my stomach, I went through the front doors. Topless girls squirmed on poles, each one like a worm on a hook. Men sat at the bar, consuming the women with their eyes, looking unashamedly over their sweating hi-ball glasses. A proud busty woman in a low-cut shirt showed me to the manager's office. He sat behind a cluttered desk in a tiny office in back, surrounded by pictures pinned to the walls, calendars and posters of the women he exploited.

"So, you want work?"

"I need it, yes." I said, with a lump in my throat.

"Well. Turn around then," he said, sizing me up like a butcher drawing white dotted lines with his eyes on a newly slaughtered heifer.

I twirled around, feeling like that stupid girl again. But I knew what was on his mind this time. I wasn't that same stupid girl anymore. This was a different kind of stupid. "All right. Good. Well, I can't put you on the schedule quite yet, but I like you. Maybe you'd be willing to do some pictures for me first?"

"I don't know…"

"I'll pay you three hundred dollars. For an hour. Tops. Easy money. No nudes. Just lingerie. It'll be real classy. I promise."

"Okay." Three hundred dollars would get me by for another week or so. I needed the money.

"You available today? I need to get you some things to wear. We'll do the shoot here."

"Yeah. Okay."

He drove me to a lingerie boutique, picked out some outfits that made me blush to look at—see-through black lace, thongs… "real classy."

The shoot didn't go as well as he had hoped. He wanted me to be nastier, more seductive. I was blank. My come-hither looks were like grimaces.

When the shoot was over, the manager said, "All right. I'm a man of my word, so I'll pay you. But you're gonna have to loosen up. I got a girl can't come in tonight. You fill in for her and we'll see. Try not to disappoint me. I'm takin' a chance here. Lots a girls'd kill for this opportunity, you know."

Yeah. He was a real philanthropist. I came back at the appointed time. All I could think about was that picture of Max through the window. It had been seared into my memory. If this is what it took to get him back, I would go through with it.

I didn't really know what to expect. Backstage, I was greeted by the House Mother, the same woman who had led me to the manager's office. She told me to get undressed, to put on some different bottoms: neon silk.

The girls talked a lot backstage. Every single one of them was troubled—drugs, alcohol, abusive boyfriends or husbands… Every last one of them had daddy issues. From the outset, I wanted to distance myself from them. I wanted to feel like I was better than they were. But I really wasn't. Most of them felt as dead-ended as I did. Many of them had become lesbians—filled with hatred and fear—as if the strip club "gentlemen" accurately represented the whole race of men. And maybe they did. I had met few good men. Very few. It wasn't that unlikely that these women had never met one. Not a single one. And perhaps the men I thought were good really hadn't been tested. Maybe I hadn't known them that deeply. Looking up at the shining world from the bottom, the whole thing looked hopelessly broken all the way up.

I left my pantyhose on underneath my underwear. Even though they were sheer, they gave me the smallest feeling of modesty. I needed that feeling.

Then it was my turn to walk on stage.

I was thankful for the bright white lights that obscured the men. Thankful for the loud thumping music that almost drowned their animal calls. But my heart jumped and skipped like it was exposed to view, like it was a fish flopping helplessly on the shore. My blood was like sawdust. I felt the fever and the chill, my cheeks blushing. I was being raped again, prodded on all sides by the violent gaze of faithless men—all oath-breakers and cowards. *I'm doing this to get Max back. Just get through it.*

I moved my puppet body, my limbs on strings—a mechanism,

a toy. None of this meant anything. Just accidents. Particles colliding. Nothing. *Give up. Nothing.*

On my break, the House Mother noticed my panty hose.

"Did you wear those out there?"

"Yeah."

"I hope no one noticed. Take them off before you go back out." There was a note of tenderness in her voice. She had to be tough, but she felt sorry for every one of *her* girls. Her foster daughters. Her lost orphans.

The manager gave me a full-time job there. Some days I worked doubles. It was miserable, soul-eroding work. If you can even call it work. I found myself unable to care about most things, like every time I took my clothes off, they pulled a little more of me off with them. Eventually, only one thing remained—that bright center of my world, Max.

I began to spend time with the girls I worked with. One of them in particular, just out of high school. I kept telling her that she didn't have to choose this life. I felt like *I* had no options. But didn't she have the whole world in front of her? She said her boyfriend wouldn't let her quit. They needed the extra income. Another woman there, Victoria, let me stay with her. I was grateful. It meant I could save more money.

I was finally able to hire a lawyer. I called her almost every day to check on my case. And every day, she'd say pretty much the same thing—*We've filed a petition... a motion... blah blah blah. We're still waiting on blah blah blah.* Legalese. A month and a half later, I'm in the same spot. In the same shameful job. Still saving. But making no progress toward getting Max back.

Victoria offered to let me stay with her until I got my own place. But I didn't want to get my own place. I didn't want to settle in. I wanted to get Max back and fly far, far away.

Victoria knew a man in the juvenile court system in Orange County. He may have been a public defender. Or the D. A. I can't remember. I don't even know how Victoria knew him. He was probably a regular at the club. Like I said—hopelessly broken all the way up. She had talked to him about my situation and he had told her how I could get Max back pretty much as soon as I wanted.

I put the plan into action right away. Another girl from the club, Kristen, agreed to help me out. We made sure Robbie and Max were both at home, then I went to his door. Kristen waited in the car around the corner. I knocked on the door. My throat had dried up from nervousness. Robbie's head appeared; he barely cracked the door open. *Here goes nothing.*

"What do you want?" Robbie said.

"I'm here to get my son."

"Says who?"

"Says me. I'm not gonna let Max turn out like you. And I'd like to see you try to stop me." I started to push by him.

"Nice try, Akeela. Go home."

He blocked my way. I pushed him. He pushed me back, coming outside. I wasn't even getting under his skin. Then I heard my mother's words in my mouth, and his face started to change.

"Such a big man. You proud of yourself?"

"You're one to talk. I heard about where you're working now. Slut. Good luck getting Max back in court."

"Oh? Are you jealous? That you just couldn't do it for me? You just weren't enough. And now you're with that dumpy little drunk whore. What was her name? I don't remember. Aww. How sad."

"You're the whore. Don't talk about her like that."

"Or what, big man? I bet you're not even enough for her *either*," I said, poking his chest with one finger. *Come on, Robbie. Hit me.* "You're such a coward. Why don't you call your little drunk out here to protect you then. Yoo-hoo!" I leaned around him to call inside. He barred my way with his arm and pushed me back. I had to press harder.

"Oh, is she out? I wonder whose prick she's sucking for a drink right now." I was channeling my mother. This felt wrong. *Whatever it takes, Akeela.*

"Shut up!" He spit in my face and pushed me back hard. I wiped his spit from my cheek, invigorated with a confidence I had never felt before. I was almost there.

"I was right to call her a whore. That's what our customers say anyway. 'If you just wanna look, go to the club. If you just wanna screw, go to Robbie's house.'" He pushed me to the ground this time. *There you go, Robbie.*

"Shut up!"

"But you know how guys are. They don't care that much about looks when it comes to sex. I wonder how it feels for your girlfriend to know that so many of her lovers are imagining someone else when they're with her. How about you, Robbie? Who do you think about?"

He slapped me in the face hard, putting me flat on my back. He jumped onto my stomach and started to throttle my neck.

"Just shut up! Shut up!"

I started seeing red. Time slowed. My arms against his chest were going limp. I think he would have killed me if two police officers hadn't shown up. All part of the plan. They pulled him off of me by his arms, releasing his choke hold.

"Calm down!" they were saying. One of them held Robbie back with one extended arm. The other helped me up gingerly.

"Are you okay?" he asked in a firm, quiet voice.

"Yeah. I just came to get my son, and he attacked me." I started to sob. "This just isn't a good place for a baby. You saw how he is. I'm trying to leave him. But he won't let me."

"And your son is inside?"

"Yes… And our passports. And my son's birth certificate." I explained where they were.

"Why don't you just come in with me, ma'am?"

While they pushed Robbie's head down into a police car, he kept screaming out, "Don't you let that bitch into my house! That's private property!" Not helping his case. I went in with the police officer. I found Max in a pack-n-play and my heart sunk. My little boy with food all over his face in a dirty onesie with a bulging diaper that was barely holding together. It had leaked out onto his onesie, so I took all of his clothes off and wrapped him in a blanket. I grabbed all of our papers and left Robbie's house. Kristen met me in the front yard.

"Can you take the boy now?" the police officer asked.

"Yeah."

"You have a car seat?"

"Yes, sir." We thought of everything. Kristen had called the police to report domestic violence as soon as she had seen Robbie's face at the door. My only job had been to get Robbie to attack me. The plan had worked flawlessly.

I walked Max over to the car. His weight in my arms, and his warmth. His eyes. I felt all over again what I had felt holding him on his birthday. A new beginning. I felt full and content again for the first time in months. I didn't regret all that I had done. I had no choice. I felt good about it even. After a whole life of waiting on others to do the right thing for me, I had finally just done the right thing for myself. I had taken my life in my own hands. Finally.

I WISH I COULD TELL you that my life just kept getting better from that point on. In some ways, it did. I worked the day shift at the club to put food on the table. Max was in a better day care facility. I spent time with him in the evenings. That was our time. The best time.

Then I met James. Max was about two and James clicked with him immediately. Victoria had a new boyfriend who didn't like me and my baby living at "his" house. Apparently it cramped his abusive nature some. So Max and I started spending more and more time with James at his place.

James looked like Elvis—a little over six feet tall, with black hair, a mischievous smile, and shy brown eyes. I liked him for loving Max. It surprised me that James would be so good with him, and I loved James mostly because I thought Max needed a father. They played together well—piggy back rides and tickle fights, all the things I wanted to see Max doing with a man. I cared for James because of Max. I had no idea at the time that James cared for Max because of me.

From the beginning, he liked having us at his house. I could tell he was already jealous for our time. We did everything together. I started to feel that familiar itch. A little voice told me that James was too possessive. Too controlling. But I ignored that voice. I wanted to do what James wanted most of the time, so it wasn't a problem. James was the best thing that had ever happened to Max. He treated Max like his own son already.

After several months, Max and I had moved in with James. He hated that I worked at a strip club, and he didn't want me to do it anymore. He wanted to take care of me. He wanted me to meet his parents. I knew what this all meant.

I wanted to make a good impression on his parents. All the clothes I owned were more fitting for the life I had been leading than the life I wanted to lead. On the day we were scheduled to go over to his parents' house, I went to a shop to see what kind of conservative looking clothes I could find for cheap. I spent too long thinking it out. James finally called the store after a few hours. His exact words to the clerk were, "Tell her to get her ass home."

James was on edge the whole way to his parents. I had never seen him like this. When we got there, we were greeted by his dad Andy, who was great. James's mother hadn't come home yet. Andy treated Max like a grandson immediately. I approached him cautiously at first.

"Max," I said. "This is Mr. Andy, James's father."

"No, no," Andy said. "Call me Papa Dobbs. I insist."

"Okay… Max. This is Papa Dobbs."

Then James's mother showed up. Vickie. She kissed James on the cheek, a sort of air kiss for Mommy dearest that kept her makeup unsmudged. I could tell already that we would not get along. She was stuck up and I wouldn't be good enough. She hated me immediately. She assessed me with her cold eyes and found me irreparably wanting. She looked at Max like he was a wart on my face.

After the cold introduction, she sat down to talk to me.

"And how old are you, Akeela?"

"Twenty-one."

"And Max is two? So young to have a child. That must be so difficult." She said it without feeling, like she had just read a statistic about unwed mothers. She took over as woman of the house as soon as she entered.

"Do you want a drink, James?"

"Sure, Ma," he said.

"You don't have to get him a drink," I said. "I'll get it."

"No. He's our guest. I know how he likes his drinks, and I

don't mind doing a little work. You sit here and rest. You look tired."

It wasn't lost on me that she had included only James in the guest category. She had already removed me from the picture. And it just went on from there. James wasn't himself when she was around. He spoke more harshly with Max and had no patience with him. I had never seen him like this. He was demanding of Max what Vickie had demanded of him: perfect outward compliance. This shattered my vision of James. He was weak-spirited. He was kind in that Iraqi way—the powerless way.

And the situation got worse. Vickie, seeing that she might be replaced by me in her son's life, doubled her efforts to be involved in every aspect of his life. This, by extension, affected me and Max. And I got fed up with it.

I liked James, but I liked him without his mother. So I made him choose. I told him I was moving back to England with Max. He thought about it for a while, then he asked me to marry him. He told me he would follow me to the ends of the earth.

James is a hopeless romantic type. He has no mind for money, business, or the practical day-to-day interactions that form the foundation of a healthy relationship. He's the kind of guy who would risk his life to spray-paint your name onto a water tower or highway overpass, but then would gripe at you the next morning because you forgot to get him frozen waffles with blueberries in them. He had a disconnect between love as a feeling and love as an everyday practice. Coming to England was a magnificent gesture, and James would do it to prove his love for me, but *living* in England was a different story.

James didn't realize how much he was taken care of. His mother still bought his clothes and sent him food. His dad paid for his truck. James lived the life of a spoiled child in many ways.

But he refused to let me and Max go. He had "Max" tattooed on his arm. He was going.

So we moved in with my mom again. I know. But I couldn't let it go. I longed for my mother's acceptance. And she was the only one of my parents that would have anything to do with me. My father had kept his word. I had called him to ask for help when I was trying to get Max back. My mother had suggested it actually.

"He's still your father," she had said. "He'll want to help. You'll see."

She was wrong.

"Max? Who is Max to me? I already told you. I have only one daughter. Don't call me again. You're dead to me."

Anyway, my mother loved James from the beginning. He was good at listening and at telling grand stories. He was good at being a son. He treated her a lot like his own mother, showing her deference and treating her like the most important person in the room. My mother appreciated being needed.

I had agreed to marry James. I assumed it would be some time in the future, and I didn't want to break his bleeding heart. I took care of all our finances in England. I found us a place to live. James gave up on practical things easily. He made excuses for himself. So I picked up the slack. What else could I do? I felt like he looked to me now to be his mother, and it was easier for me to fulfill that role than to teach him how to be a man. What did I know about that anyway? His mother had done a real number on him. He never really grew up.

I worked three days a week and went to school four. I finished the university program in a couple of years. I felt like I had been working non-stop the whole time. I didn't know what else to do but continue my schooling, so I applied to a law school program.

I figured it would be easier for me to do my own legal work. Between custody battles and divorces, I had already spent a lot of time in court, and a lot of money on lawyers. And I didn't really trust anyone. Better to take things into my own hands. I had good grades and excelled in every area but math. I had to take a remedial course and pass an exam before the law school would approve my application.

In the meantime, I kept working at a designer clothes store while James played Mr. Mom. He did odd jobs here and there to make a little extra money. His parents also sent him money and gifts. Of course.

My future career in the law rode on this one math exam. I waited for the school to get back to me, but they were waiting until the last minute. Two weeks before the program started, I was still waiting on a response.

Then one day, James came into the store, all sweaty and winded. He had run there with a manila envelope in his hand. He yelled for me as soon as he got through the doors, "Kee! Kee! It's here. It came!"

All my fellow employees crowded around. I had been griping for weeks about how I couldn't wait to hear back about my application. And now the moment had come. I opened the envelope carefully, taking my time. I pulled the letter out and read the first few words, "We are pleased to inform you…" I had been accepted! Not only that, I had been granted a full scholarship for my tuition, and they had approved loans if I wanted them so I wouldn't have to work. Filled with the excitement of this triumph, I left work right then, hopped on my bike and carried the letter to my mother's house. Nothing I had ever accomplished had made her proud. But surely this was something. Surely now, she would see how hard I had worked… how valuable I was.

When she came to the door and saw me, still catching my breath, my face flushed, she asked, "Keela. What's wrong with you? What happened?"

"Mom…" I paused to breathe a bit. "I got in! To law school. I got a full ride! Everything's paid for. I got in, Mom! Can you believe it?"

"Jesus, Akeela, is that it? Anyone can do that. All you have to do is show up, right? I thought something terrible had happened. You scared me half to death."

I was crushed. Again. I should have known better. But I still clung to the naïve belief that if only I tried a little harder, if only I could do a little more to please her, that I would finally gain her acceptance. I left her house, feeling completely deflated. James had planned a big celebration party, but my heart wasn't in it. What was there to celebrate? James got really upset with my mother when he heard what she had said. But nothing he did now could help me regain that significant feeling my mother's cavalier dismissal had taken from me. Again.

My plan was to marry James before I started law school. We had been organizing everything on a shoestring budget for months. Some girls in the design program at the university had offered to make my wedding dress for the cost of material if I agreed to model for a few of their fashion shows. I negotiated and wrangled for everything else. And our wedding was still gorgeous.

I felt like this was my first real marriage. I felt like I had been coerced into my marriages with Firaz and Robbie by force and circumstance. But I had chosen James. Hadn't I? It was hard for me to tell anymore. You get to a certain point in your life when you have been thinking about yourself and other people in a certain way for so long that it doesn't feel like you have a choice anymore. About anything.

Andy and Vickie came to Manchester for the wedding. That was an added stress. James stayed with them almost exclusively when they arrived. He would kiss me on the forehead and say things like, "You don't mind, do you babe?" while he was already pulling away from me to meet up with his parents.

I had no one to help me get ready on the day of the wedding. My father had nothing to do with me as I expected, but my mother wasn't there either. She wanted to look good for the wedding, and spent most of the day on her own preparations. She even tried to borrow a formal dress from me for Layla. She was upset that I didn't have one to borrow and that I didn't have time to work out any other options. Layla didn't want to be in the wedding for some reason. I had recently reconnected with Allison, so she agreed to be my maid of honor. A couple of girls from school were also in the wedding. But none of them were there to help me prepare. I started to feel sorry for myself a little.

Then Angela showed up. When I had moved back to England with James, she had called me. She wanted to meet James. I was cold toward her.

"I know what you said to my mom, Aunt Angela."

"I don't know what you're talking about."

"About how you were having to raise Max all by yourself. How I needed to do my part. How I needed to pay for the consequences of my own actions. You remember now?"

"Akeela. Dear. I never said those things. I would never... That explains a lot though. I was wondering why you had cut me out of the loop. I promise you I would never say that. I didn't feel that way at all. Your mum said I *should* feel that way. But I didn't. I told her you were doing the best you knew how."

My mother. I couldn't understand what could have made her

this way. But I was glad to have a relationship with Angela again. If not for her, I would have been alone on what should have been a happy day for me. If no other day is a woman's day, at least her wedding day should be. I had already had two wedding days that weren't my days. This was shaping up to be my third until Angela arrived.

She brought me shoes and gloves and jewelry. I remember looking at her face in the mirror as she helped me with my hair. I felt like she had filled in as my true mother. She even kept Max while James and I went on our honeymoon.

And the wedding was lovely. Even Vickie couldn't find fault with it, though she tried. I was ready to tack the "happily ever after" onto my fairy tale ending. But not so fast.

After James and I had been married for a few months, his parents came out for a visit. The love between me and James had already dissipated. I thought his love for Max would be enough. He thought his grand shows of affection should have bought him my enraptured and undying loyalty. But I didn't want a husband who did grand things, really. I just wanted one who would do the little things. Who would take care of things without being nagged. Who would work hard and keep me, protect me. James just refused to grow up. Our relationship ran hot and cold. Mostly cold. And when Vickie showed up, everything came to a head. James and I split up, and she convinced him to move back with her to the States. He said it was so he could find work—"Isn't that what you want from me, Kee?"—but it felt more dire than that. I didn't expect to see him again.

I MUST PAUSE A MOMENT. Perhaps you are becoming as weary with this story as I am. It dragged on like this for quite some time, but what can I say? This is my life. I thought things would be different when I escaped from Iraq. It was easier for me to deal with the pain and tragedy of my life when someone else was shoveling it onto me. In those times though, I still blamed myself. I had blamed myself that my parents rejected me. That I had been raped. I had taken all of that on myself even when it wasn't really my responsibility. Now, I had freedom to choose my own course, yet I couldn't see how my choices were destroying me. The situation had reversed. *Then,* the responsibility had been someone else's, but I had taken it on myself. *Now,* the responsibility was mine, but I felt like a victim of circumstance. And it didn't get better.

James called for me to return to the States, so I went. He had adopted Max. Didn't Max deserve to at least see his father? I wanted to believe a person didn't need a father, but I knew this wasn't true. Hadn't my father's absence left a hole in me? All the girls at the strip club had daddy issues. So they rejected the need for men altogether. But the hole was still there nonetheless. Some of them thought they could fill that hole if only they could find the love in another man they had never had from their fathers. And most men are all too willing to trade some imitation tenderness for sex. I wanted to believe I was different. And if I couldn't be different, I would make things different for Max.

So we traveled back and forth between England and the U.S. I was trying to gain for Max what I had lost. I had little hope I could gain it for myself ever again, but I kept trying anyway. How I kept trying I have no idea. Why wouldn't I just give up? Like my lungs and heart that just wouldn't quit, I had a drive, almost autonomous from me, that just wouldn't stop trying to gain acceptance and satisfaction. No matter how many times I failed, I kept going back for more. They say insanity is trying the same thing over and over again expecting different results. I was insane then. But what could I do? I couldn't rely on anyone else. If I stopped trying to rely on myself, what would I have then? Wasn't that just another name for *dying*? So my heart kept pumping blood. And my spirit kept longing. But I couldn't hold onto anything. No matter how hard I tried, satisfaction fled from me. As did love.

Vickie had gotten James a dog. He had enrolled in college. Also Vickie's fault. It was obvious he had no plans to return to the U.K. He had settled in. If I wanted to make this relationship work, I would have to move to America. I would have to take care of things, just like I had done throughout the rest of our relationship. James said I could transfer to Stetson University. He wanted me back.

"Come on," he'd say. "Let's give this just one more shot. For Max."

So I did. Because, remember, I'm insane.

JAMES SAID HE WOULD GET us a house before I moved out there. To my great disappointment, though not to my surprise, James did nothing to find us a place. His mother had convinced him that we should stay there. James, the dutiful son, had complied. But he hadn't told me because he didn't want to upset me. He hadn't wanted to do the legwork to find us a place anyway. Now, he didn't have to do anything. I think his mother thought she could split us up for good if we stayed there. I was determined not to give her that satisfaction.

As soon as we moved in, Vickie went to work alienating me. She regularly spoke about me in the other room, just loud enough to make sure I could hear every word.

"Why does she have to go everywhere with you, James? Why is she even here? She's so clingy. You've hardly even been studying.

She's holding you back."

Needless to say, this couldn't last. We got our own place. Vickie had lost the battle, but I would lose the war. James couldn't handle the stress, like his divided loyalties were ripping him in two. He started to crack.

One evening, we ate dinner at his parents' house, like we often did. And his mother started up, like she often did.

"Now, James. Make sure you take home some leftovers. You look so thin. Are you even *eating* at home?" She shot me a glance, like James was wasting away and it was all my fault.

"Yes, mother," James replied.

"Well, that's all right. They probably don't even know how to make real mashed potatoes where she comes from. So who can blame her?"

"What is that supposed to mean?" James said. "*Where she comes from?*"

"England, dear. I was talking about England."

I couldn't stay silent any longer. "Mashed potatoes were invented *where I come from*. And mine are just fine, thank you."

"I didn't mean anything by it," Vickie said. "No need to lose your temper."

"Oh, you'll know if I lose my temper. I'm not even close," I said.

"I'm sure that's a real sight to see. I can't wait," she retorted.

James's face had been darkening the whole night. While his mother and I were staring each other down, he swiped his full plate of food off the table. The plate shattered on the floor, drawing Vickie's and my attention away from each other.

"James! What on earth are you doing?" his mother exclaimed.

"I'm tired of this, Mom. You're always criticizing Kee. There's nothing she can do right. You've just been nothin' but a..." He paused in unfamiliar territory. "But a *bitch* since you met her. And I'm sick of it. Come on, Kee. Let's go."

On the way home, we hardly said a word. I was thankful he had stood up for me, but this James was one I had never seen before—brooding, unpredictable, thin-skinned. He stayed that way. With me and with Max. Like some switch had been flipped. His mother didn't come over anymore, and James started to blame me for that. And for everything else that went wrong in our lives. James still had to borrow money from them, and it was only a matter of time before his mother rushed in to save him from me. I was so weary. I don't know if I had ever been refreshed.

We started seeing a counselor together, but that didn't last. James was so jealous. When the counselor told James to leave the room so he could ask me some questions in private, James responded, "What, you wanna fuck her too?" He wanted me with him at all times. He was terrified of being alone. Even more than I was. And he invested in that fear so much that it made me want to leave.

Then one night, James and I had a huge fight. I can't remember the exact circumstance, but the argument eventually came around to the fact that I was tired of being his mother. I thought I was telling him the hard truth—you know, tough love. It didn't work out the way I had imagined. After our discussion had escalated into a shouting match, James pulled a butcher knife on me and held it to my throat. I had threatened to leave him. He had his arm around me. He spoke into my ear, sobbing.

"You can't leave, Kee. I need you."

"James," I said as calmly as I could. "What are you doing?"

"I don't know." His voice in my ear quivered pathetically.

"James, this is not working out. I'm done. I want to leave. Just let me go."

I gently pulled his hand and the knife away from my throat and pulled away from him. He didn't resist me. He slumped to his knees, breathing heavily and crying quietly. Then he flashed the knife to his own throat.

"James," I said.

"You wanna leave? Go then. What's the point? You just give up on us like that? 'Cause it's all about you, right? But if you leave, I have no reason to live." He started to cry again, closing his eyes and tensing his body at intervals, like he was readying himself to slit his throat. I backed away from him, got Max, called 911, and left the house, hoping he would be alive when the police got there. They came and took him away. They put him on suicide watch in isolation for seventy-two hours. The police told me I should leave while he was away. No problem.

BELIEVE IT OR NOT, THINGS hadn't quite reached rock bottom for me. By this point, I had been through so much, it didn't even register as tragedy anymore. This was just my life. But I wanted something better for Max. I realized it then. Every time I tried to do good, bad came of it. Was I a mistake? I didn't seem to fit in anywhere.

Not long after I left James, I met Rob. Another Rob. It was as if the universe were screaming in my ear—*It's the same guy! Run away!* It's easy for me to see that now. But I didn't see it then. I had broken my promise to myself. I had never really searched my heart to find out who I really was. Not knowing who you are doesn't mean your life stays on hold. It keeps right on flowing. And when you don't even know who *you* are, it's easy to be fooled by others.

I met Rob in Daytona. At the races there. He was freshly divorced, raising four sons by himself. He figured out immediately that the way to get to me was through pity. And he was very persistent. He lived in Georgia, but he came down to visit me every other weekend after the races. And every time he visited, he had a new tale of woe. He was doing his best, but the boys needed a mother. That kind of stuff.

I really had nothing to live for but Max, and he needed a father. Didn't he? It seemed like a good match. I could be a mother to his boys. He could be a father to Max.

A few months went by, and Florida got hit by back to back hurricanes. There were tornadoes and storms too. A whole slew of natural disasters.

Rob called me to say I should just come stay with him until things settled down in Orlando. He said I could come and meet his boys. It was an appealing offer. I was tired of putting gasoline into a generator just to have power. A line had fallen into the swimming pool out back, so sparks flew from the surface of the pool every time I flipped the breaker just to microwave a frozen burrito. It was miserable. So I decided to take Rob up on his offer. He flew down, got a rental car, and drove me and Max and our stuff up to Georgia.

Things at Rob's house were not good. Without a mother, the four boys had completely gone to seed. The house looked like it had suffered its own string of natural disasters. Rob had hidden much from me on his visits. Like the fact that he was a drunkard for one.

My pity for Rob felt sometimes like love. After ten days at his place, I was pregnant. I know. As soon as I told Rob I was pregnant, it was like the facade hiding his world just dropped. He knew it would be hard for me to leave now. So he stopped fronting. It was scary. He was a drug dealer. A compulsive gambler. And a porn addict. I think he had exposed his boys to porn in some misguided Neanderthal attempt to make men out of them. The youngest boy used to sneak into the bathroom while I was in there to stare at me. He stared at me at night while I was sleeping. I told Rob about it, very concerned. After a "That's my boy" kind of grin, Rob told me, "That's just his way of getting close to you." But I understood the boys. Like I understood Susan the paraplegic. Like I understood the dancers at the strip club. People in pain seemed to gravitate toward me. I understood what they were going through. I knew what it was like to grow up broken and suffering. I knew what it was to be a victim.

I took the kids to counseling. I tried to make things at home normal. At least what I imagined normal to be. And everything was great. Until Rob came home. He was cruel and moody when he wasn't drunk or high. Violent, loud, and inappropriate when he was. He gambled away all our money. Excuse me, *his* money. And I caught him looking at pornography regularly. He didn't even care if I caught him.

He would say something like, "Come on, baby. What does it matter where I get my appetite as long as I eat at home?"

He didn't realize how inadequate I already felt. I was pregnant and feeling bloated and ugly. Did he not realize how his porn addiction made me feel? Was it my fault? Was I not sexy enough for him? I certainly didn't feel sexy. And you can say I shouldn't have cared. But I did. I wasn't going to leave those kids there with him alone, so I tried to make the best of the situation. Rather than helping me to make the best of it, he just took advantage of my helpless situation.

I REKINDLED A RELATIONSHIP WITH my mother halfway through my pregnancy. Perhaps I was stupid for thinking things would work out differently with her, but I needed to believe our relationship was fixable. If change wasn't possible—real lasting change, then I was doomed to do to others what had been done to me. But I didn't want that. I didn't want to be a hurt person hurting people. I had to keep pursuing my mother. Maybe I married the same kind of man that many times for the same reason. I needed to believe real change was possible. But no matter how hard I tried or how many times I renewed my efforts, the outcome was always the same. Failure. My hope in lasting change was fading.

When Lily was due, my mother came to see her born. Lily was bigger than Max, and I'm narrow, so her shoulders got stuck. The doctors sent everyone out but Rob. They all had concern on their faces. I had lost a lot of blood. When they sent my mother out, she said something like, "What's the big deal? She's having a baby. Not dying." But she became much more worried when the minutes turned into hours and she still hadn't heard any report of success.

Eventually, she went nuts. She started screaming from the waiting room, "She brought me out here on purpose! And now she's shutting me out. She's punishing me!" That kind of stuff. She yelled so loud, I could hear her from the delivery room. One of Rob's roughneck friends finally shut her up. I heard he took her by the throat, pushed her to the wall, and said something like, "Shut your mouth. This isn't about you. When she's done, you're gonna go in there calmly, and you're gonna act like you care about someone other than yourself." That was the polite version. His version had more cursing. He and Rob laughed about it a good bit later.

My mother never gave up on her bitterness toward me. She acted somewhat civil at the hospital—on a leash. But as soon as we got home, she let me have it.

"How dare you bring me out for this? You could've died and they wouldn't even let me in the room. Your own mother. And who is this man you've married. Seems like a real bastard."

All the same stuff. But I was done hearing it. I never should have waited so long to be honest with her. When you wait too long to say the things that have hurt you, sometimes they rot inside you. And even though what you say eventually may be true, it's too late to do any good. It just wounds. I told my mother all the things I had wanted to tell her for years. She took it badly. And we haven't really talked since. Just like that, and my parents didn't exist to me but in bad memories.

Things with Rob got even worse after Lily was born. He beat me, threatened me, and yelled at me and the kids all the time. I remember locking myself in my car with Lily and Max while a drunk Rob banged on the windows threatening to kill me if I left. I didn't want this for Max or Lily. I needed to get out. But he had isolated me. I wasn't allowed to have friends. I wasn't allowed to work.

One morning, I woke up feeling a little nauseated. A little *pregnant*. A test confirmed it. I did another. Same thing. I was going to have another of Rob's children. You may be wondering at this point how I was able to sleep with this man. As if not sleeping with him were an option. But it was a combination of things. It kept the peace at home, what little there was to be had. Anyway, I was pregnant again. And I knew I could never leave Rob now. Not with another child binding me to him. I told him that night.

"Rob, I'm pregnant." I figured the straightforward approach was best.

"What? You sure?"

I showed him the test.

"Dammit. Why'd you go and do that for?" he exclaimed, throwing up his hands. "Well, you're gonna have to take care if it."

"What do you mean?"

"I mean I don't want no more goddamn kids. Hell, I don't even want the ones I got. I sure as shit don't want another."

So I had two choices. Take my kids and start walking—with no place to go, no car, no friends, nothing. Or have an abortion like he kept insisting. Did I think it was right to kill my baby? No. But I didn't feel like I had a choice. I knew nothing of the whole process. I hadn't thought about it.

Rob took me to a clinic in Atlanta. It reminded me of that clinic in Basra. A little more modern and sterile perhaps. But all the clients had the same look on their faces. Like they should be afraid of everyone who looked at them. After Rob had paid, they gave me two pills in a plastic cup. To help me relax. I had to give them a urine sample. Between my mental state, the guilt, and the medication, I don't remember much.

The doctor, or whatever she was... I mean, I don't think she was holding up much of the Hippocratic oath... she thought I was probably too far along for a pill. She wanted to make sure. She ordered an ultrasound. I remember seeing that black and white screen in my hazy state. I heard the watery blips, the insistent beat of a tiny heart. The baby was far enough along to tell the gender. A boy. I realized then even through my medication what we were doing. We were killing someone. Rob acted like it wasn't a big deal. I think he had done this before.

"So, as I thought," said the doctor, "the pregnancy has progressed too far for a medication abortion to be effective. It might work, but probably not."

"What else can you do?" Rob said. "I don't wanna have to

come back."

"I would recommend an in-clinic procedure. The most common type is aspiration…"

She talked to Rob. I felt like she barely even looked at me. She continued.

"It shouldn't hurt much. About as much as menstrual cramping. She'll have to wait here for an hour after. Then you can take her home. She should come back for a check-up in a week or two. You can set that up before you leave. Any questions?"

"No," said Rob. "Let's do it."

I watched myself being brought into a room. They set my feet in some stirrups. It was like I was giving birth. I heard a machine turn on, whirring loudly. Someone pressed down on my stomach hard, and they shoved a tube up into me. She hadn't been right about the pain. It wasn't much different than childbirth for me. There just wasn't anything lovely waiting on the other side of it. I heard the sounds, grisly and gurgling, like something wet and clumpy being sucked up into a wet/dry vac. The whole thing took ten minutes. There was no dignity in this. What had I done? *Shut it out, Akeela. You did what needed to be done. Nothing. This is nothing. Just particles. Accidents. Nothing.*

Rob took me home an hour later. He acted relieved. He pretended to be understanding. "You did the right thing, babe. You did the right thing."

I just couldn't believe that. I had been lied to. I had wanted to believe the lie. Wasn't it easier this way? What else could I have done? Did that matter? This was the worst thing I had ever done. Someone had suffered again because of me. Had died because of me. Another lamb had died in my place. Why? Was it not enough that I suffered? I despised myself. Looking in the mirror made me sick. Looking at Rob was like looking in the mirror.

I have never gotten over it. And it was settled. I would leave Rob no matter what it took.

ON THE WAY HOME FROM the store one day, I passed by a fitness center that had just opened up near our house. I was a certified trainer at the time. I don't think I told you about that. I have loved exercise since I was young. It was easy for me, and it got my mind off of things. In law school I had started training people on the side, and eventually it just took over. I dropped out of law school and got certified in physical fitness instead. I loved helping other people get fit, especially women. It seems to come easily for me. This was real change, was it not? Change for the better? For most, the change was not just in their bodies. I saw how it improved marriages. How it made people more confident. People talked to me. They shared their troubles. I could empathize. I felt like this was just what I was meant to do.

So I stopped in at this new gym and applied for a job, and they hired me pretty much on the spot. I had to tell Rob about it, and he was not happy.

"What? Now I've gotta bring home the bacon… and then fry it too? Who's gonna take care of the house?"

"I'll take care of it, Rob. I can do both."

He finally capitulated, but we fought about it a lot over the next few months. He didn't want me to gain my independence.

I saved everything I made. I wanted desperately to get out of that house. Lily was a year old. I felt like she had already seen things no child that age should have to see, but she was also getting to an age where she understood more of what was going on, and that terrified me. Would she accept this reality as normal? Rob's boys cared about me, but they were going Rob's way and there was little I could do about it. I had given up on Max having a dad. Rob was certainly no role model. Everything I had ever tried had come to nothing. I needed another new start. Maybe that would make the difference. The owners of the gym had the most beautiful marriage I had ever witnessed. They loved each other unconditionally. How they acted toward one another in front of clients and how they acted in private matched up. They were who they were all the time. I didn't believe it at first, and I found myself watching them, looking for a rift—a little crack that would expose what was really going on underneath the superficial happiness. But I never saw anything. The husband, a tall, handsome, muscular man, had women throwing themselves at him every day. But it never fazed him. He treated the female and male clients with the same friendly professionalism. He glowed with his wife, and with no one else. I wondered what made them so different. Eventually, I just asked him. And he told me.

"Jesus. He has made all the difference."

This stunned me a bit. I hadn't thought much about God or Jesus. All the American Christians I had known were hypocrites. But this couple was different. I couldn't put them in that same category. Their love seemed more real and more constant than any love I had ever experienced. It gave me hope.

When he invited me to church, I refused at first. I was not churchy. Church was for good people, right? For people who hadn't seen and suffered what I had. But the husband kept persisting. Every other day or so, he would say something like, "You should come to church with us. Bring your family."

I felt like maybe there was something to this church. These people were real. And they were good. The only reality I had ever known in people was bad. I believed that. I believed people were bad. I had never seen anything much to convince me people could be good. Until now. So I decided to give it a try.

Rob and all the kids came with me that first Sunday. Rob criticized the church from the beginning: "A bunch of hypocrites. They think they're so much better than us." But I didn't see it that way. My boss was for real. So I started to go every week, but Rob refused to go again. Well, he didn't outright refuse. He just always had some excuse after that. His boys followed their father's example. So I started going with Max and Lily.

I worked five days a week, and on Sunday I felt for once like a normal person. A few months passed. One Sunday, a new family joined the church. My boss, who sat next to us, leaned over to me, seeing something unsettled in my eyes.

"Kee, what's wrong?" he whispered.

"I don't know. I have a weird feeling." I whispered back.

"Do you not like it here?"

"No. That's not it at all."

"Then why don't you join too? You've been coming long enough."

I shook my head.

"What's wrong, Kee?" he whispered, a little more urgently.

"I don't know. I just have a weird feeling in my stomach."

"Like a pull?" he offered.

That was exactly what it felt like. The exact word. A *pull*.

"Yeah. Exactly," I said.

"I've had that before. We'll talk more about it Monday, okay?"

On Monday, he brought me into his office. He wasn't going to let it go. I felt a little badgered. A little gnawed on. He kept on and on about Jesus this and "personal Savior" that. Then he opened a piece of paper he had been clutching the whole time. It was a version of the Sinner's Prayer. I had said it before.

"I've already said it. It didn't work."

"You didn't really believe it," he replied.

"Well, how do I just believe it now?"

"Would you try? For me?"

"Fine. But I'm not promising anything."

I knew a lot more now than I had. I honestly felt like I had never done anyone wrong on purpose. I felt like the things that had gone wrong in my life were not really my fault. If that were the case, why had I blamed myself for them before? I couldn't say. Maybe I wanted to exercise some control over them. I didn't want them to be out of my hands. Perhaps I thought that through suffering I could gain acceptance. I had heard the verses. About the need for a sacrifice to atone for my sins. These verses made sense to me. Had I not been my own sacrifice, though? Had I not suffered enough to pay for at least myself? How much could I possibly be worth anyway? If I had been up for ransom, no one would have paid a dime to release me. What had people called me? What had I called myself? *Damaged goods. A stripper. A whore. A baby killer.* When I compared what I was worth with how much I had suffered, I felt like the balance was in my favor. I didn't have a debt to God and others. I had a *credit.* But then why the Cross? I didn't want anyone else suffering for me. I didn't even feel like I needed it. I wasn't worth it, for one. And I had already paid. It didn't seem necessary.

Yet people suffered because of me anyway, and I kept suffering too. I thought of my children. I thought of that tiny boy whose beating heart had been stopped. I thought of my parents. Of Angela. Of the people who had done me wrong. Of all the abusers punishing what they saw of themselves in the world. Of all the schemers trying to jostle their way to the top. My suffering was not my own. It was everybody's. No matter what I did to try to contain it in myself, it spilled out. No matter how much I tried to block and drain it, it kept raining down from above. Suffering covered the whole human race like a shroud. I knew it. I had seen it. And I knew that no matter how much I suffered, no matter how hard I tried, nothing would ever be good enough. I couldn't blot out my own suffering or anyone else's. I had blocked it for years. I tried not to remember it. I couldn't face it. And even if I faced my own life and blotted out the sins *against* me and *in* me, the suffering of the world would just find me again. If I were to be raised up out of this, my salvation would have to be bigger than just me. It was out of my hands. What the church said had been true. Salvation is of the Lord. Or it doesn't exist. Did God have the power to raise me from the dead? Even me? Could I become like the glowing people I saw at church? It seemed impossible. But I felt that pull—that unborn hope in me quickening. It had been leading me and searching me as I read the prayer. And then I stopped reading the prayer, and I started praying it.

THINGS DID CHANGE AFTER THAT. They got *worse*. I had expected that my transformation would be instantaneous. That my problems would just melt away. It didn't happen that way. I don't think it ever does. I felt like I had been sold a fairy tale. Believe in Jesus and you can have that "happily ever after." Christian music and Christian movies sell that message. But it just isn't true most of the time. Or *any* of the time from what I've seen.

A year or so passed. I started reading the Bible a lot more, and I found that I had more in common with the people in it than I had with the people at church. Joseph and Job stood out to me particularly. My boss told me this was just Satan trying to test me. Well then Satan had been testing me my whole life. I thought believing in Jesus was supposed to end that.

I started seeing people at church in a different light. I got baptized and joined the church soon after I prayed the Sinner's Prayer. Then, and only then, people who had never even looked at me came up and hugged me, welcoming me to the church. I just didn't see Jesus in that. Jesus would have hung out with a woman like me. The Samaritan at the well—the half-breed whore. Jesus didn't wait for her to believe before He treated her like a human being. And maybe this was Satan tempting me, trying to cause me to doubt. But there was more.

I had saved enough money to move out of Rob's house with Max and Lily, but he turned our divorce into a protracted and miserable ordeal. He had a live-in girlfriend a week after I moved out, and she was a hateful vindictive tramp. She contacted me on Facebook and cursed me out in a message that was also sprinkled with condemning Bible verses. I couldn't figure that one out. I told her as politely as I could to stop bothering me. Then she got Troy's number somehow and called his flat. His girlfriend picked up, and this crazy woman called her a "nigger lover"! I couldn't understand why she hated me so much. Wasn't the betrayed *wife* supposed to be the one with all the righteous indignation?

One day, I was pumping gas, and she showed up at the station. She started yelling at me and running toward my car. I took a few steps toward her and she froze. Still yelling. I knew she didn't want to get in an honest fist-fight with me. That would've ended badly for her. I felt my rage welling up in me though. This woman wouldn't leave me alone.

Finally, she yelled out at me, "I know what you did! You were having some other man's baby, and you forced Rob to pay for an abortion. You filthy whore! Baby killer!"

She drove off. I sank down into my car. He had lied to her. He had twisted her up. My anger vanished and pity replaced it. That poor woman. But there was more.

Rob still had visitation rights with Lily. And Rob's girlfriend made sure to use Lily, who was almost three, to try to get back at me. She would send Lily home with a boy's hair cut. Or with make up smeared all over her face like *Toddlers & Tiaras* meets Heath Ledger's Joker. They didn't take care of her when she was there. Her diaper area had developed a rash that seemed to get worse with every visit.

In preparation for the divorce, I started to do some research on Rob. Even given my already low opinion of him, what I found shocked me. I had the passwords for his e-mail accounts, and I found his membership information for numerous porn sites, as well as adult "friend" finders. He had been paying to meet up with underage girls. I saw his profile picture and my heart stopped: he had Lily sitting on his lap. He was soliciting sex online and his profile image had my little girl in it. I thought about Lily's rash, and I became sick. *No, God! No!* I couldn't believe it. I didn't want to believe it. But every week that Lily came back from a visit, her rash didn't improve. And I started to think it wasn't a rash at all.

At the prompting of a friend, I asked Lily about it. She could talk a good bit, but I assumed she wouldn't know what was going on.

"Lily, princess?"

"Yes, mommy?"

"When you stay at Daddy's, does anyone touch you… in your diaper area?"

"Yes."

"Who?"

"Daddy."

"At diaper time? Or all the time?"

"All the time."

I was losing my nerve. *Just keep going. For Lily.*

"Baby, how does he touch you? Where does he touch you? Would you show mommy? Touch me how he touches you."

She lifted her middle finger and put it to my crotch. And right there, I lost what little faith in God I had. Burned away. I could take this myself, God. But Lily? My little baby? I thought you would make things different now. I thought I would be one of the normal people now. You were supposed to protect me. But no. No one was going to help me. Hadn't I already known that? I had to take things into my own hands.

I took Lily to the ER and I filed a claim with Crimes Against Children. No one believed me. I showed them the pictures of Rob's profile. They said I could have had those made. I had his passwords after all. I was just a jilted wife trying to get revenge on an innocent husband. I had but one hope—that the court would rule in my favor and I would be free from Rob forever.

But the case just kept dragging on. I talked to my boss.

"Things have only gotten worse since I believed."

"I keep telling you, Kee. This is Satan's way. You know the parable of the sower? Before you were like the hard-packed ground. Satan and his demons just plucked up the seeds of truth from your life. But don't be like the seed in the weeds or the seed in shallow ground. Don't let the cares of life or trials destroy your faith. You have to keep believing."

"This may seem wrong to you. But I feel like I've always believed. I've always held out a hope that everything in my life happened for a reason. But what has it ever gotten me? You don't know where I'm coming from. You were raised in this. You've never had to suffer like I've suffered. It's easy for you to believe. Don't talk to me like you know."

"Then tell me."

"Look. I can't. I can't do this anymore."

"Okay." He paused for a long time. "I'll pray for you."

I stopped going to church. These people weren't real. If God just touched them with affliction, every one of them would turn their backs on Him. I had come to God from tragedy hoping for resolution and comfort. But He had repaid my trust with only more pain. So He didn't exist. Or He was cruel. Those seemed like the only options.

ROB HAD MONEY, SO HE hired the best lawyers in the county. My lawyer was the best I could afford. I had never known the Rob that showed up for our hearings. He was calm and respectful. He wore a sharp suit that covered his tattoos. All of it seemed very natural. My testimony seemed dishonest in the face of his contradictory presence. He had everything organized and explained. I was distressed. I would get hysterical. I had no peace. I was desperate. Rob's lies seemed true. My truths seemed false.

Rob had turned his boys against me as well. Whenever I showed up to visit, he told me they weren't there. He told them I didn't want to see them again. I had never felt more alone. The night before the final hearing, I came completely undone. I had no one. I could do nothing. I would probably lose my daughter. And then what? I couldn't let that happen, but everything I had done to force the issue had only made it worse. I had offended God. I had rejected Him. But I had no other options. I got on my knees. I would try one more time. I started talking. About everything. I opened up old wounds. I let myself bleed. I let myself go.

I gave You my life. I gave You my son's life. I should hate You. I should hate everyone. But I don't feel hate. I feel disappointment. I feel betrayal. I wanted so badly for You to be real. To fix everything. I've tried to do everything right. I've followed my heart. I've lived a better life than most of the people that claim to follow You. And

You haven't even tested them. They have easy lives. They stress over how they're going to pay the mortgage on their McMansions. About Johnny's hangnail. They tell me to have faith. But they've never really had to exercise any. And You know I've tried to believe. What are You trying to teach me with all of this? Well, You can stop now. I think I've learned it. You've taken everything from me. Everything. Can't You hear me? I have nothing. Every time I have even the smallest shred of happiness, You snatch it from my hands. But it doesn't matter. I've already said You can do what You want to me. But my children? Why? Why do You make them suffer? Why do You make anyone suffer? I gave them over to You. But I'm not willing to let them go. Is that it? Is that the lesson? You want me to just trust You? Well, You have a fine way of gaining my trust. How can I trust You now? I've been beaten over the head by all the church mice. But why should I believe in You? They have their reasons, but none of them have seen what I've seen. Why should I believe the stories? I'm supposed to forgive my family like Joseph did with his brothers? I'm supposed to keep my mouth shut like Job? I'm supposed to forgive all these abusers and schemers and helpless bystanders like Jesus did on the cross? But I'm not like them. I've tried to be. I've tried to be like Jesus, but all I've ever felt is His suffering. All I feel is His rejection. But I don't feel anything else. Don't take my little girl. Oh, God. If You're there, listen to me! I know I can't do anything to fix this. Please! You're the only one who can get me through this. I'm not asking for a miracle. I just want to know You're here. With me. I want to know that You've been with me. Let Rob's true colors show tomorrow. Please God. Is that too much to ask? I just want everyone to see who Rob really is. Show me You're there! God. Please. Just show me You're there.

I pled with God most of the night. As my prayer continued, a strange thing happened. For the first time in my life, I felt like I was really talking to someone. I felt like God was right there in the closet with me. Even to this day, I think back on that night and I think maybe I did the wrong thing. Did I put God to the test? I don't know. But I was honest with Him. More honest than I had ever been with myself. I had finally dug up all the resentment and bitterness, the pain and the suffering, and I dumped it on Him. I wasn't carrying it around anymore. I could see my past clearly now, but I wasn't afraid of the truth anymore. I wasn't afraid of who I was anymore. God had taken my fear and my pain onto Himself. He became my scapegoat that night. I trusted in Him completely for the first time. And He gave me peace.

I DIDN'T KNOW WHAT TO expect the next day. I felt peace about the situation for the first time, that same peace, and I looked with charged expectation for God to show up and answer my prayer: *Do not let those who trust in You be put to shame.*

The time came for the hearing to begin, but Rob hadn't arrived. His lawyers kept calling his phone, but no one got any answer. Their messages became increasingly animated. The judge said the hearing would have to be postponed if Rob didn't show up within the hour. *Please, God. No. I want this to be over.* Rob's main lawyer was obviously irritated. His tense voice spit into his phone: "Look, Rob. If you don't get your ass down here in the next thirty minutes, I'm giving them whatever they ask for, so help me God."

Rob eventually showed up. He had been at work. I could hear his voice out in the hallway yelling. His lawyer went to meet him. Rob started laying into him.

"You didn't tell me anything about this," Rob yelled.

"This has been scheduled for two months, Rob. Where have you been?"

"I've been at work trying to make enough money to pay your

sorry ass. I thought you were supposed to tell me about this shit."

"I did tell you. Like I said, this hearing's been scheduled for two months."

"Like hell it has. That bitch has been…"

The bailiffs came out into the hallway and interrupted them.

"Hey! Keep it down. The judge is ready to begin."

Rob walked into the courtroom. Oh my. He wore dirty cutoff jeans, work boots, and a yellowed sleeveless T-shirt. All his tattoos were showing. His face was cocky and angry. He looked like a bulldog chewing on a wasp. When he saw me, he started to run at me, so I ran in the other direction, out the side doors of the courtroom. He followed me yelling. The bailiffs lagged a little behind. When they found us, he had backed me into a corner. He was screaming in my face.

"This is all your fault. You fucking cunt. You set this whole thing up. Well, I hope you're happy. You're not getting a goddamn dime!" The bailiffs pulled him away from me. "Not a goddamn dime!"

I didn't fear him. In the least. I felt completely calm. This was God answering my prayer. I could feel it. I knew it was true. God was there for me. What did I have to fear if I knew He was working this out? I went back into the courtroom.

"Are you okay to proceed, Mrs. Green?" the judge said.

"Yes, your honor."

"This is great," my lawyer whispered in my ear.

"Mr. Green?" the judge said. Rob had leaned back in his chair with his dirty boot up on the table. Some red clay had knocked out of his tread. He was picking his nails defiantly.

"What?!" Rob exploded.

"Mr. Green. Control yourself."

"Hmph."

The judge kept peering over his reading glasses at Rob, who had never been more himself in public. It was like he was possessed.

"What's the resolution then? What are you asking for?" the judge said to my lawyer.

"My client wants full custody of the child and child support. She accepts her car as alimony."

"That's all? Do you accept these terms, Mrs. Green?"

"Yes, your honor."

"Do you have any paperwork drawn up?"

"Yes, we do," my lawyer responded. Rob's lawyer started blustering.

"We haven't seen anything, your honor. We have not agreed to any terms. We'll need to review…"

"Let me see it," the judge interrupted, still talking to us, basically ignoring Rob and his lawyers. My lawyer brought the judge the papers.

"I need a few minutes to look these over. We'll reconvene in half an hour."

After court reconvened, the judge sat in his bench, put his arms on his elbows, folded his hands, and turned to Rob's lawyer.

"I'm in full agreement with these terms. I think you'll find they are quite fair for both parties."

"This is bullshit!" Rob said, letting his chair legs drop loudly to the floor.

But he signed the papers. He had little choice. And it was over.

My lawyer walked me out to my car.

"It's over, Kee. Don't worry. I'm staying here until this thing is signed, sealed, delivered, and filed. I'll make sure of it." He paused. "And yes. You have your life back."

His firm waived my remaining fees—about seven thousand dollars. My lawyer said it was the least they could do after all I had gone through. I was free. Truly free. I got in my car and closed the door. I paused with my head down, just enjoying the silence and the peace. A few weeks before, I had found a miniature New Testament outside my car. I had set it in my coin holder. I looked down at it now. It was the final token of that day. A kiss from God. *Thank you, God. For everything.*

So do not lose the courage you had in the past, which has a great reward. You must hold on, so you can do what God wants and receive what he has promised.

Hebrews 10:35–36

Epilogue

M Y COUNSELOR TOLD ME ONCE that my life is a story of betrayal. I don't believe that. I know the majority of this book has been a sad story. Believe me, I know it. It's my life. Some people suffer because of the choices of others. Some suffer because of their own choices. I've suffered from both. I still wonder why God put me through all of this. But I no longer question His goodness in it. I'm part of a much bigger story. And that story is not one of betrayal. It's one of redemption.

Some people say God doesn't care if we're happy. I don't think that's true. He just doesn't want us to settle. A good parent will take things from his children. Most children would be happy eating candy all day long. But that's not good for them. It doesn't really satisfy. The child doesn't know as well as the parent what's good for him. And we don't know as well as God. For me, God kept taking one rotten thing after another out of my hand, and I kept taking up something else. And the whole time, it was like He was saying, "Kee, I've got something to give you that's better. Just hold on for a minute." But I wouldn't even wait to receive it before I snatched up something else. I needed to come to Him empty-handed. Every time I have placed my trust in something other than God, He has taken it away. I see it in my whole life. Long before I put my trust in Him, He was drawing me to Himself. He loved me first.

If God hadn't taken so much from me, I wouldn't have Max and Lily. I wouldn't have found Jesus. I wouldn't be helping people. I know I'd be a stuck up princess looking down my nose at everyone. But I've been at the bottom of society. I know what it is to be deformed of spirit. To loathe your own face. I know what it is to be an orphan. I know the hearts of women who sell their nakedness to survive. I know what it feels like to think you have no other option but abortion. I know what it is to be completely powerless. I've seen the darkness in my heart. I can't think I'm better than anyone. I know I'm not. But I would not have learned that lesson the easy way. I'm too stubborn.

I once thought my life was unfair. I realize now that I got what I was asking for. I wanted justice. But I should have been asking for grace. It wasn't until I was honest with God and with myself that I realized that. I had become so afraid of becoming my parents. All I knew was who I *wasn't*. But I didn't know who I was. Or who I wanted to be. I was so afraid of being alone, of having nothing to hold on to. Fear. It dominated my life, but I tried to fake it. I would say I had given up. I said it so many times. But I didn't trust God. So I hadn't really given up. I would trust people and they would let me down. I trusted myself, and I proved untrustworthy. But when I fully trusted God, I found peace. I am no longer a victim of circumstance. I know the circumstances of my life are in His hands. And I know He cares for me as a true Father. The one I never had. And as a true Husband.

I know that, I say. But I'm not going to lie to you. Sometimes that doesn't feel like enough. Does having a heavenly Husband keep me warm at night? Does having a heavenly Father mean I don't care that my earthly father hasn't spoken to me in years? Of course not. But I'm willing to wait on God. I know He'll give me those things in the right way when it's the right time. I'm not taking any shortcuts anymore though. Do I want the comfort of a man's arms so much that I would be willing to place that desire over God? That's a struggle. But I'm thankful that God always checks me when I start to desire something more than Him. I have a plaque in my room that I try to live by: "A woman should be so lost in God that a man must seek God in order to find her." I've given everything to God. I trust Him. He'll do right by me.

This story started bubbling to the surface again after that first night when I was honest with God. I had hidden this story from myself and I had lost myself in the process. I had blocked everything in a futile attempt to spare myself. I thought I could be good enough to merit acceptance with my mother, my father, my friends. Even God. But all I got for my effort was pain, so I tried to own the pain, like maybe suffering could be my highest virtue. But no matter how much I suffered, I felt only more forsaken. More unforgiven.

I had such a low estimation of my value and significance. I didn't trust what God said about me. He said I was worth the life of His Son. And He doesn't lie. That means at least two things. For one, I can't pay my debt. No matter how much I sacrifice. No matter how much I suffer. No matter how many good things I do. It will never be enough. But it also means that God values me so much that He would give His Son for me. I can't pay for myself because I'm more valuable to God than I ever could have imagined. I have to remind myself of that a lot. Sometimes I still don't understand *why* God would love me. But I know He does.

Why tell this story? My hope is that one person out there gains some comfort from what I've gone through. From what I've learned. That wouldn't be possible if this were all senseless tragedy. It might look like that sometimes. But it's not. I feel like God has been with me even when I haven't felt His presence. When I look back at my life—at all the details that came together to bring me to this point—I realize that God has had a hand in it all. Just like with Job, God knows exactly what I can take. And what I need.

So many times in the midst of tragedy, we look to ourselves. "Why me?" we say. But our suffering isn't always just about *us*. Jesus didn't suffer for Himself. He suffered for others. And when we turn our lives over to Him, we suffer for others too. My hope is that the suffering I've endured might be of benefit to others to help them trust God even in the hard times.

If you're a Christian, I hope this book encourages you to be real. With yourself, with others, and with God.

If you don't believe in God, I hope you've developed a better excuse than I had. If anyone has had a good reason to deny God, it's been me. And I don't think it's something special in me that allowed me to see Him. I think anybody that looks can see God working. If we're being honest.

This has been a difficult story to tell. And the story isn't over really. I never got that storybook existence. All the frogs I've ever kissed have stayed frogs. Prince Charming never showed up. No "happily ever after." This is a true story. But I've learned a secret about reality. It's better the way it is. I've spent enough time wishing for something I don't have. I'm looking forward to heaven, but I don't have to wait until then to find satisfaction and contentment. Or happiness.

Because I'm not just surviving now. I'm finally living.

Feedback and Questions

If you would like to leave feedback about this book or ask a question, please visit

IfILiveToTell.com

THANK YOU!